Model Housing

From the Great Exhibition to the Festival of Britain

MODEL HOUSING
From the Great Exhibition to the
Festival of Britain

S. MARTIN GASKELL

An Alexandrine Press Book

MANSELL PUBLISHING LIMITED,
LONDON & NEW YORK

This book is part of the series
Studies in History, Planning and the Environment
Series editors: Professor Gordon E. Cherry and Professor Anthony Sutcliffe

First published 1986 by Mansell Publishing Limited
(A subsidiary of the H.W. Wilson Company)
6 All Saints Street, London N1 9RL
950 University Avenue, Bronx, New York 10452

This book was commissioned, edited and designed by
Alexandrine Press, Oxford

Printed in Great Britain at the Alden Press, Oxford

British Library Cataloguing in Publication Data

Gaskell, S. Martin
    Model housing: from the Great Exhibition to
    the Festival of Britain.——(Studies in
    history, planning, and the environment)——
    (An Alexandrine Press book)
    1. Labor and laboring classes——Dwellings
    ——Great Britain——History
    I. Title   II. Series
    728.3   NA7552

    ISBN 0-7201-1834-4

Library of Congress Cataloging in Publication Data

Gaskell, S. Martin.
    Model housing from the great exhibition to the
festival of Britain.

    (Studies in history, planning, and the environment)
    "An Alexandrine Press book."
    Bibliography: p.
    Includes index.
    1. Housing——Great Britain——History.   2. Dwellings——
Great Britain——Design and construction——History.
3. Architecture, Domestic——Great Britain——History.
I. Title.   II. Series.
HD7333.A3G37   1986   363.5′0941   86-23775
ISBN 0-7201-1834-4

Contents

Preface

This book sets out to survey the model house as a design feature during the period from 1851 to 1951, concentrating on both the changing expectations of housing over this period and the changing response of architects and designers to the requirements of society.

It is concerned essentially with model designs for working class houses, and deliberately isolates those designs and schemes put forward as 'models' of their kind, in order to emphasize what people at particular points in time considered to be 'models' of design. These represent either an ideal to be aimed at or a considered response to existing conditions. With such an emphasis, it is hoped that this study will allow the identification of the factors affecting design and influencing, in terms of housing, style, layout and accommodation provision.

Over the period from 1851 to 1951, the survey includes a range of housing types – tenements, flats, rural cottages, bye-law houses, municipal housing, as well as houses proposed in architectural competitions and in journals and magazines. In its approach to these various building types, the book endeavours not only to examine the designs for individual buildings, but also to evaluate these against the broader environment within which such proposals were put forward.

The model house is a very useful and productive vehicle for approaching design history. At specific points of time it enables one to examine the origins of different attitudes and approaches to design, and allows one to consider how people over a period responded to economic conditions, how they sought to reflect changing attitudes and ideas in design patterns, how they incorporated technological developments, and how they translated contemporary stylistic ideas and innovations into practical design possibilities for different social groups. The book is presented, therefore, as a study, in one aspect of design history, of both changing attitudes and changing requirements during a period of exceptional economic and social progress. Hopefully it will also provide an introduction to the roots of much subsequent housing design.

The contents of the book fall into three parts. The first section on the concept of the model house provides a definition of the term model housing, an historical background with respect to attempts at design and provision, and an indication of the issues which such a study raises for the design historian. The central section of the book consists of a series of case studies, each of which involves a description of the particular project, a commentary on its design features, and extracts from contemporary material. The final section on the impact of model housing concentrates on the way in which the designs of such houses have reflected changes in style and attitudes as well as changes in social and economic circumstances. It is concerned, therefore, both with the development of ideas as well as with the practical development of housing.

This book derives from a range of work undertaken over many years on the history of housing and town planning. I have been fortunate during this time in the advice and criticism I have received from a number of friends and colleagues, especially Theo Barker, Martin Daunton, David Stenhouse, Michael Harrison, Steven Jackson, Paul Laxton, John Marshall, Anthony Sutcliffe, Mark Swenarton, Jennifer Tann and Robert Thorne. I am grateful for the opportunities of working with students on the History of Design course at North Staffordshire Polytechnic, with whom I have been able to discuss and develop many of the ideas and issues involved in this subject. Above all I am obliged to Peter Green for initiating the idea of this study and, personally, to Graham Davies for his interest and involvement throughout.

S. Martin Gaskell
City of London Polytechnic

Acknowledgements and Sources
of Illustrations

The author and publishers would like to thank the following for permission for the use of material quoted in the text or for use of illustrative material.

In case study 9 to J.N. Tarn and Cambridge University Press for permission to quote from Tarn, J.N. (1973) *Five Per Cent Philanthropy: An Account of Housing in Urban Areas between 1840 and 1914*.

In case study 13 to M. Swenarton and Heinemann Educational Books for permission to quote from Swenarton, M. (1981) *Homes Fit for Heroes*.

In case study 17 to the Trustees of the Mass Observation Archive, University of Sussex for permission to quote from Mass Observation Survey (1943) *Enquiry into People's Homes*.

In case study 18 to the Controller of Her Majesty's Stationary Office for permission to quote from Ministry of Housing, Housing Advisory Committee (1944) *Design of Dwellings*.

In case study 20 to M. Banham and B. Hillier and Thames and Hudson for permission to quote from Banham, M. and Hillier, B. (eds.) (1976) *A Tonic to the Nation*.

On page 27 to the British Architectural Library for permission to reproduce the illustrations.

On pages 33 to 34 to the Greater London Photograph Library for permission to reproduce the photographs in its possession.

On page 52 to Manchester City Library for permission to reproduce the photograph from its Local History Collection.

Sources of Illustrations

Below are the sources of the illustrations according to the pages on which they appear:

page 20: *The Builder*, **IX**, 1851; page 22: Roberts, H. (1851) *The Model Houses for Families*, London; page 27: Society for Improving the Condition of the Labouring Classes (1851), *Plans and Suggestions for Dwellings*, London; page 32: *The Builder*, **XXX**, 1872; page 33: photograph in collection of *Greater London Photograph Library*;

page 34: *ibid*; page 36: *The Builder*, **XXI**, 1863; page 36: *ibid*; page 40: Strickland, C.W. (1864) *On Cottage Construction and Design*, Cambridge; page 41: *ibid*; page 43: *ibid*; page 47: *Building News*, **XXI**, 1871; page 51: photograph in the Local History Collection of Manchester City Libraries; page 53: photograph by Dr. D.K. Stenhouse; page 55: Meakin, B. (1905) *Model Factories and Villages*, London; page 56: Harvey, W.A. (1906) *The Model Village and its Cottages: Bournville*, London; page 57: Meakin, *op. cit.*; page 61: London County Council (1901) *The Housing Question in London*, London; page 62: *ibid*; page 66: Parker, R.B. and Unwin, R. (1901) *The Art of Building a Home*, London; page 68: Unwin, R. (1909) *Town Planning in Practice*, London; page 71: *The Builder*, **IXC**, 1905, page 72: *ibid*; page 73: *ibid*; page 77: *Town Planning Review*, **IV**, 1913; page 79: *Town Planning Review*, **VI**, 1916; page 82: Local Government Board (1918) *Report of Committee on Building Construction in connection with the Provision of Dwellings for the Working Classes in England, Wales and Scotland*; page 84: *ibid*; page 88: Ministry of Health (1927) *Housing Manual on the Design Construction and Repair of Dwellings*; page 89: *ibid*; page 91: *ibid*; page 96: *ibid*; page 97: *ibid*; page 100: Ascot Gas Water Heaters (1938) *Flats, Municipal and Private Enterprise*, London; page 101: *ibid*; page 102: *ibid*; page 105: BBC (1945) *Homes for All*, Worcester; page 110: Ministry of Housing, Housing, Advisory Committee (1944) *Design of Dwellings*; page 111: *ibid*; page 113: *ibid*; page 116: BBC, *op. cit.*; page 118: Madge, J. (1946) *Tomorrow's Houses*, London; page 119: BBC, *op. cit.*; page 122: McG Dunnett, H. (1957) *Guide to the Exhibition of Architecture, Town Planning and Building Research (Poplar)*, London; page 125: *ibid*.

SECTION I

The Concept
of the Model House

The Concept
of the Model House

The model housing concept reflects very much the concerns and commitments of Victorian Britain. It brings together a practical response to the problems of the environment and a sense of social awareness with that abiding passion for instruction and improvement. Design is placed at the service of more broadly conceived social and economic requirements.

On this basis, the model house developed in the nineteenth century and achieved an accepted architectural function in the hundred years from 1850. The model house was not to do with an unattainable ideal, but rather with the realistic alternative. It had thus a dimension beyond those of architectural creativity, patronage and philanthropic endeavour: that dimension was didactic. Those who promoted the schemes which this book will examine were concerned to demonstrate their visions in a form which others could emulate. The model as defined was to provide both a standard and example that was worthy of imitation. In the way that ideals and good practice were combined with instruction, the model house can be placed in the same category as other agencies of Victorian concern for improvement, such as public galleries and museums, gardening clubs and friendly societies, technical schools and model factories. It had all the hallmarks of Mr Gradgrind's archetypal preoccupation with practical common sense.

It was in this sense that the model house was pre-eminently Victorian, both in character and in terms of the period when it came to the fore. There had, however, been earlier examples of such endeavours and the term itself had come to be used in eighteenth-century England. Prior to then the emphasis had been on planning and the model community; houses had been of secondary importance and often incidental to a larger concept.

Model towns and villages had featured in the history of urban form in Britain since the Norman Conquest. Through them certain standards had come into operation and, in the eighteenth century, certain aesthetic expectations had achieved popularity. This practical impetus distinguishes these endeavours from the tradition of idealistic schemes with which nevertheless they have a connection. That tradition derived from Plato and, evolving through Christian humanism, found its clearest English expression in the writings of Thomas More and Francis Bacon. Their concern, however, was with a vision of perfection – the search for utopia. For Plato this was to be found through the vision of labour in a concept of functional perfection. In this ideal the city had to be strictly sub-divided to reflect the separation of social and economic functions. Such a theoretical approach had little concern for the details of the physical environment. Other than that buildings were so organized as to meet defence needs and were planned to reflect an immutable social structure, they were not in themselves important.

These attitudes continued in the tradition of thought that produced More's *Utopia* and Bacon's *New Atlantis*. Utopia's strict emphasis on equality, social co-operation and physical order was reflected in the division of its urban settlement into regular sections with uniform houses. There was little imagination in either the layout or building of these ideal cities. This moral tradition, however, was significant in terms of the context within which many nineteenth-and twentieth-century practitioners conceived their model houses. It is a theme to which reference will recur throughout this study.

The reality of model building however had its roots in a different tradition; that of British town foundation. The planning and planting of new towns started in earnest with the Norman Conquest; but what is important in this context are those occasions when individuals or governments set up models in advance of contemporary practice and as examples for others. 'The golden age of medieval town planning in Europe', as Tout referred to the years from 1220 to 1350, was one such occasion, when in particular Edward I was responsible for the foundation of more than 100 in the territories of England, Wales and Gascony.

With the advice of those who 'know how best to devise, order and arrange a new town', guidelines for this development were established in relation to the layout of roads, the width of major and minor streets, the size and allocation of plots, the provision of churches and public buildings, and the relationship of houses and gardens. Planning was of a general nature, though normally provisions were included to regulate the height of houses and to stipulate the materials for their construction. As a result the bastides of Edward I were characterized by their grid-iron layout, their division into standard house plots and the continuous frontage of houses along the streets.

Such features recurred many times in model schemes and reflect a continuing concern for order and economy. In the sixteenth century Elizabeth I's statutes incorporated notions on the distribution and occupation of houses in London which were intended to establish good practice. Such controlling models were strengthened after the Great Fire with the imposition of standard street widths and standard house types in the re-building of London. Sir John Summerson has described how the elevations of the re-built houses were divided into four classes for better regulation, uniformity and gracefulness. Building was also standardized by requiring the use of brick or stone walling and tile roofs, and by specifying the number of storeys to be built in streets of differing widths and importance. Developed and extended in relation to other towns in the course of the eighteenth century, this type of legislative control was the forerunner of the nineteenth-century model bye-laws and the government housing standards of the twentieth century.

This practical, if cautious, application of building codes was significant in that it involved the rejection of the grand design. In the immediate aftermath of the Great Fire, Wren, as well as Evelyn and Hooke, produced plans which imposed an ideal pattern on the City, reflecting the principles of Renaissance monumental architectural planning. Derived from the ideas of Vitruvius, they embodied the forms and geometry of the ideal city schemes of Alberti, Filoranti and Scammozzi. The language of their plans took hold in continental Europe in the seventeenth and eighteenth centuries and was represented in the building and re-building of numerous capital towns. England rejected this emphasis on the monumental and concern with the rational ordering of space. In doing so it turned its back on the ideal plan in favour of the more mundane work of controlling the different component parts of the town, and in favour of realizable models.

This was as much to do with scale as approach, and it is not surprising that in Britain the term 'model' gained common occurrence not in the city but in the country in relation to the estates of the eighteenth-century landed nobility. As a result, throughout the country there are hundreds of villages and settlements which owe their origin, or their appearance, to the fact that they were the planned creation of the landowning classes. Such developments were conceived of as 'models' and have subsequently been characterized as such, either because of their significance in the history of design and layout, or on account of their contribution to the improvement of labourers' housing and the quality of rural life.

In the eighteenth century such model villages gained their impetus from the improvement of both agricultural estates and aristocratic parks, when entire communities were often uprooted and re-housed in planned settlements which served to embellish the estate and, at the same time, to enhance the aesthetic appeal of the 'improved landscape'. This connection between village development and 'gardening' meant that by the late eighteenth century, as Picturesque theorists took hold of taste, estate cottages were viewed increasingly as part of an idealized rural landscape evoking traditional associations – 'the pattern of village green, scattered, thatched and overgrown cottages watched over by the church spire'.[1]

The model village involves, therefore, either the restoration and renovation of an existing settlement, or the design and building of a new community on lines which not only demonstrated the wealth and power of the landowner, but also reflected the latest tastes and fashions. Such developments were facilitated by the alterations in the traditional pattern of settlement occasioned by Enclosure and were thus connected with the practical concerns of agricultural improvement. By the end of the eighteenth century landowners were increasingly aware that having a well-housed labour force paid off in terms of improved health and increased labour efficiency, along with the corresponding decline in demand on the poor rates. To do what was fashionable was reinforced by a growing sense of moral responsibility.

The principal consideration in the first instance was the grandeur and delight of the new nobility; it was the educated and elevated Whig aristocrats, with their knowledge of European taste and culture, who translated classical architectural ideals into practical realization. As a result, the notion of the 'model' house established itself in relation to the planned community and not just in terms of the individual house. Moreover, it did so not within the urban setting but in remote rural communities.

These model villages, therefore, take building and planning into a new field; the housing of the labouring class became a matter of architectural consideration. From circa 1760 architects were required to turn their minds to the design and planning of small-scale rural communities and the type of housing previously considered as totally insignificant.

Inevitably in these circumstances the concern was to place such houses within the broader, and grander, concept of the estate and the community. It was then in terms of planning rather than architecture that these model villages broke new ground. Symmetrical formalism marked them out, compared with the haphazard individuality of the traditional village. In model estate villages such as Harewood and Lowther, Milton Abbas and Belsay, the greatest attention was given to siting and overall appearance. At Harewood the cottages are linked together by architectural features to give the effect of an urban terrace; at Lowther the projected crescents and circuses emulate the style of Wood's Bath; in Belsay the arcaded cottages reflect the neo-classicism of the house, and in Milton Abbas the unformity of elevation of the cottages complements the regularity of layout. The model was here used to demonstrate not only the control of the landed nobility over the environment, but also the way in which men of wealth and taste could bring reason and order to the living conditions of the lower orders.

In the latter decades of the eighteenth century the impact of these model villages was increased with the spread of pattern books, standardizing building forms and techniques, while suppressing the vernacular traditions. As a consequence more attention was given to the individual house and the notion of the model cottage achieved common currency. The form that this development took owed much to the theories of the Picturesque, and in the process the model cottage attracted to itself the attributes of romantic sensibility. The cult of the Picturesque was established by Richard Payne Knight, Uvedale Price, Humphrey Repton and John Nash, and as a result of their influence, by the end of the eightenth century it had become associated with features that were poetic and charming and appeared in the landscape as a sham Gothic ruin, a grotto or *cottage orné*.[2]

The roots of such activity lay in the realization of a romantic attitude to nature; a sense of exploration and self-abandon. Nature was accepted as supreme, and on that basis the theoreticians developed and analysed certain criteria of aesthetics, such as surprise, contrast and variety. In the process they raised the general consciousness of certain qualities in landscape, and established a new pictorial vocabulary which depended on the vision of the artist. Rejecting any visible control of Nature which served to stamp man's artifical patterns on the landscape, the Picturesque attributed beauty to every kind of scenery and to every object. It was thus that the humble labourer's cottage achieved its place in the application of this visual appreciation of nature in relationship to building.

This interest was further emphasized by the encouragement of nostalgia and the search for primitive virtues and innocence. If Romanticism meant escape, then it meant escape not only from the realities of life into Nature, but also escape into distant times and spaces. Such escapism sent the Picturesque traveller to the Lake District and North Wales, in search not just of the sublime landscape, but also the delights of the ruined castle or group of thatched cottages. The Picturesque was concerned, therefore, not only with architectural style but also with an idealistic lifestyle. When William Howitt reviewed the *Rural Life of England* early in the next century, he reflected this sense of idyllic pastoral existence:

> Ah! Cottage Life! . . . these rustic abodes must inspire us with ideas of a peace and purity of life, in most soothing contrast with the hurry and immorality of Cities.[3]

Domestic buildings were treated in relation to their surroundings, and thus the Picturesque encouraged the return to local vernacular styles or their equivalents. To a large extent this process went no further than the ornamentation and beautification of a gentleman's estate in the latest fashion. Out of this search for at least the impression of an idyllic pastoral existence there did, however, emerge a serious attempt to re-instate the architectural values of small-scale buildings.

This was achieved through the pattern book, developing from 1775, which translated fantasy into practicality and established the model cottage as the prototype of nineteenth-century improvement. The authors of the pattern books developed their models from the Picturesque characteristics of the village, which were defined by Price as being 'intricacy, variety and play of outline'. The aversion to symmetry which had shown itself first in gardening was related to architectural practice and building design. In the Picturesque village the cottage could never be symmetrical, while porches and windows, chimneys and eaves were exaggerated in scale and position in the search for dramatic effect. The pattern books took these features and fashions, and combined them with an increasing understanding of historical styles in order to provide, with professional skills, plans that could be followed by country builders.

While the concern was to achieve an idealized cottage style with some roots in tradition, the emphasis nevertheless was on an overlay of decoration and detail deriving from a debased sense of the vernacular and an imperfect understanding of the Gothic style. The pattern books made no attempt to provide any practical remedies to housing problems; the Picturesque was primarily concerned with the exterior rather than the internal domestic comfort of these dwellings. Deep eaves and tiny, ornate windows served to exclude much light, while patterned roofs and fretwork verandahs presented problems in terms of repair. The excesses of the first model cottages were far from practical. Nevertheless, such ventures on the part of the landed classes had considerable influence because of the extent to which their standards and fashions were emulated, and because of their subsequent impact on housing improvement.

The problems of housing the rural labourer were widespread and well known by the end of the eighteenth century. The rural slums of pre-industrial England were the consequence not only of the rapidly growing population from the latter years of the century, but also of the fact that the actual amount of cottage accommodation had contracted, owing to the consolidation and improvement of estates along with the operation of the Poor Law and Settlement Acts. Cottages were actually pulled down, parishes depopulated and migration prevented. At the same time, there was a steady upward movement in cottage rents. Sir Frederic Eden noticed that this was already underway by the 1790s; but the sharpest rise coincided with the general rapid inflation of the war years. As a result, overcrowding intensified the problems of ill health and disease occasioned by damp, badly built and badly maintained cottages with inadequate drainage and sewerage. Large families forced into inadequate accommodation occasioned mounting concern over their intemperance and immorality.

Information on this situation was available by the end of the eighteenth century in the reports of the Board of Agriculture and in the writings of local parish ministers and egalitarian reformers. There was a beginning of an awareness that bad housing could endanger both physical fitness and life expectancy. The direct correlation of the quality of housing and the productiveness of labour in truly a Benthamite sense did not gain full expression until the 1840s. There was, however, particularly during the Napoleonic wars, a developing sense of the value of housing as a positive agent of social control. Cottage improvement was strongly urged by individuals like Frederic Eden and Nathaniel Kent, and in the Agricultural Surveys of the Board of Agriculture issued in the war years.[4] In 1797 the Society for Bettering the Condition of the Poor was established with the principal objective of improving the domestic comfort of every cottage. Closely allied to arguments for the provision of gardens and allotments, the subject of 'model cottages' was firmly on the agenda of public debate by the beginning of the nineteenth century when the Board of Agriculture offered for the first time a prize for the best plan of a model cottage for a rural labourer.

As a result of this interest, a handful of landowners was actually involving itself in the provision of such housing. The motives of those who built model cottages were far from simple. What is important is that by the late eighteenth century the architectural and aesthetic impetus was being paralleled by a practical concern arising from an appreciation of the debilitating effects on the labourers of a poor home environment. Whether this was stimulated by charity or commercial common sense will be a question that continues throughout the history of model housing.

By the early nineteenth century, then, the term 'model housing' had not only come into fairly general usage, but had become associated with certain features that were to characterize its development and its contribution to housing reform and improvement from 1850 onwards. The main feature of the model house was that it was conceived of as 'an improvement', and it was created either in plan or reality to demonstrate how that improvement could be achieved. Such improvement could be concerned primarily with either the appearance of a house, both individually and in relation to its community, or the quality of the building, in terms of layout and provision of accommodation and of soundness of construction. The importance of model housing was that it brought these two concerns together in a combination of practical knowledge and aesthetic consideration. This meant that model housing was not only something that was planned and preconceived, but that it was seen very consciously in terms of demonstrating to the lower orders what was considered 'good' for them. Inevitably what was 'good' for them was also of interest and benefit to their betters.

Thus model housing began in the eighteenth century in relation to the improvement of landed estates; in its subsequent development, in the nineteenth century, it became a possible form of individual munificence and an element in civic responsibility and regeneration. As such the model house reflected fashion both in matters of style and standards. In its concept, however, it differed from the ideal house in that the model house was something that was realizable within the financial constraints and circumstances of the time. In these ways model housing served to reinforce current economic and social values. It was not an alternative utopia, but a demonstration of the way the domestic situation of the working classes could be improved within the economic expectations of society. As a result, model housing could be innovatory, but more commonly it served to reinforce contemporary values and attitudes.

This quality is seen very clearly in the range of material encompassed within this study. The late eighteenth-century interest in estate cottages carried forward into the next century. Landowners sought to improve their estates, while agricultural and housing reform societies regularly sponsored designs in the hope of alleviating the housing conditions of the labouring class. The problem that bedevilled all these efforts was the practical consideration of building cheaply enough to provide a cottage that could be let at an economic rent which the farmworker could afford.

This conflict between what was desirable in terms of appearance and proper building standards, and costs was central to the development of model housing. With the pressure of urban growth and industrialization, the problem of workers' housing had extended from the countryside, and overcrowding, dirt and disease characterized the housing of the rapidly growing towns of Victorian England. The realization of the need for improvement, which stemmed from the reports and investigations of the 1840s, was recognized in the housing reform movement, which formed a significant force for social improvement over the following 100 years. Architects brought forward model designs; individual industrialists and philanthropists promoted model buildings; societies and organizations encouraged the working classes to seek their own model solutions.

Through all this activity eighteenth-century notions of community were not forgotten, and there were numerous efforts to place the model house in a broader context and to restore traditional values through the creation of model villages. Originally conceived of in relation to a works or an industry, such model villages took on an identity of their own in the garden villages of the late nineteenth and early twentieth centuries. From then on the model house cannot be separated from the layout of its environment, ranging from the model estate to the model town. Inherent in that process was the increasing impact of national and local control.

The use of external regulations to impose minimum standards had a long tradition in Britain. During the course of the nineteenth century all towns and cities developed their local bye-laws which conformed increasingly to the standard of model codes promulgated nationally. From the first decade of the twentieth century such control was combined with the control of the urban environment as a whole. The minimum standards for model estates and model towns, as well as model homes, were now contained in government legislation. Good practice, as disseminated through official publications, was reinforced by the possibility of financial penalties. Model housing thus became official; it had not lost, however, those essential qualities of instruction and improvement which had always characterized it.

These qualities mean model housing cannot be isolated from either the architectural or the social context. In the period 1850 to 1950 this meant, in the first place, a background of both changing styles and changing technical facilities. The very notion of the model house had had its gestation in the Romantic search for the vernacular cottage, which in turn contributed to the Gothic Revival of the early nineteenth century, as the follies of eccentric patrons gave way to the 'Gothicizing' of country houses, and the building of new Gothic mansions and villas. By the middle of the century the attributes of Gothic architecture had been related not only to the dwellings of the well-to-do, but also to those of the poor, at least when conscious thought was given to their improvement. A style that carried with it moral as well as artistic values was inevitably seen by some as the most appropriate form for the regeneration of working class life. Pugin's *Contrasts* were applied to contemporary requirements.

Such application did not, however, isolate model housing from the battle of styles that raged after 1850. The merits of the classical form of the terrace as compared with the individualized cottage were debated in the Victorian architectural press and demonstrated in various model schemes; the contrast was most sharply drawn in the urban, particularly metropolitan, setting when model dwellings took the form of tenements and substantial architectural edifices. The reaction to this High Victorian monumentality was to have consequences for both the form and style of later Victorian housing. The revival of the English vernacular and of craftsmanship in building in the last third of the century was realized in the picturesque work of Baillie Scott and the dream-like houses of Lutyens. The style that characterized *Das Englische Haus* not only influenced housing of a lower order, but was also based on certain qualities which the promoters of model housing sought to inculcate.[5] As a result, the vernacular revival and the cottage movement of the late nineteenth century became closely associated with the Garden City idea and the town planning movement of the early twentieth century. At its worst this degenerated into the sham Tudor of the speculative builder; nevertheless, it placed the individual house firmly within the context of the planned community.

Beginning before the First World War, but with growing impact between the wars, architects and town planners became increasingly involved in the provision of working class housing. This was to provide well-built and well-planned traditional houses in settings that evoked England's rural heritage. Such housing was grounded in an attitude set in tradition. Model housing of this period, for all its achievements was tied to a utopian dream of a pseudo-medieval past. A new generation in Britain after the First World War wanted an architecture that belonged to its own time, and that took account of steel, concrete and glass, as well as the potential of machines. Inspired by the work of Le Corbusier and the idea of *La ville radieuse*, architects of the Modern Movement were concerned to place housing within a broader functionalism, and to design units of housing within an extended environment and in relation to the overall planning of population distribution. Within this approach, the concern was to exploit new materials, new equipment and new methods of building. With the rise of modern architecture, not only was there a new battle of styles with regard to housing design, but also a renewed debate as to the social force of such provision.

Model housing could never be divorced from the social context in which it took effect, and over the preceding century the expectations of society, as evinced in social reform and legislation, had both changed and expanded. In 1850 it was only beginning to be recognized that the physical environment of the urban poor was not inevitable, and that the conditions under which they lived were not necessarily of their own making; nor could they be cured by the poor themselves. Rather some form of public intervention and control would be required.

Throughout the preceding two decades a series of government enquiries, along with the work of medical reformers and statistical societies, had made public the conditions in which the poor lived and, in particular, the problems being created with the shoddy new houses being thrown up in many developing urban centres. These reports were concerned primarily to identify, investigate and publicize the dirt, disease and squalor which the rapid growth of towns had intensified to a level which threatened social stability.

As a result, by 1850 working class housing had become a 'problem'; but as yet a problem that was to do essentially with sanitation and disease. From there on the pattern of ideas with regard to housing reform developed in a series of well-defined spurts. The intensity of interest in the subject kept pace with the changing degree of practical activity in housing reform, which stemmed from both commercial and philanthropic sources, and later from public as well as private finance. Despite the widespread interest of the 1840s, it promoted limited activity during the following decade, although urban areas continued to grow in size, and overcrowding in some central districts was increasing. The 1860s, however, saw a revival of interest in housing reform, largely inspired by the achievements of promoters of model housing. This decade witnessed a renewal of concern for the problems of urban life, and a steady growth of general interest in the problems relating to the laying out of estates and the planning of houses for the working class. The need to make provision for light, air and space in the layout of housing was an idea that was increasingly promoted throughout England from the 1860s and 1870s onwards, and was to secure legislative expression in the Public Health Act of 1875.[6] This new awareness of spatial requirements produced ideas and concepts which, combined with the growing movement of population to the suburbs, promoted the novel approach to housing layout that characterized the latter years of the nineteenth century.

Alongside this change in awareness of the needs of working class housing during the second half of the nineteenth century, there was a corresponding evolution of public responsibility in terms of the role that government, both local and national, should take in the reform of housing. The example both of reforms that had been achieved and of powers that had been taken to control the worst excesses of housing speculation persuaded those in authority of the benefits of positive action, as distinct from merely responding to an unsatisfactory situation. This change in attitude was reflected in the willingness, on the one level to set controls over building as brought forward in the model codes and bye-laws of the 1870s, and on the other to initiate the clearance of slums and the building of dwellings for the poor.

None of this was achieved simply or directly; the interference of government was finely balanced with the interests of property. Nor did it remove the housing problem. That was recognized by the Royal Commission on the Housing of the Working Classes of 1884. But what was also recognized was that henceforth it would primarily be the state and the municipality which would operate to raise minimum standards and to finance housing provision for those people that needed it. This was acknowledged in the Housing of the Working Classes Act of 1890, which enabled municipal bodies to extend their interest in housing beyond that of simple demolition and reconstruction, and to become land purchasing and house building agents.[7]

The opportunities opened up by the Act set the parameters of debate for the twentieth century, between those who wanted local authorities to take all possible action to remedy social evils, and those who were alarmed by the potential effect of the growth of municipal power. House building and reform became a factor in local politics and, as this development coincided with the general acceptance of housing reform as part of the broader concept of town planning, brought both the type of housing as well as its means of achievement into the forefront of public debate. But though this was given impetus in the 1909 Housing and Town Planning Act, it does not mean that there was an upsurge of house building before the First World War.[8]

As throughout this period, there was limited correlation between times of ideas and initiative and times of action and achievement. Real results in housing were limited, then, before 1914. After the war, however, the country embarked on the provision of council housing as a regular means of accommodating working people. This meant, to some extent, the acceptance of subsidization, the refusal of which had bedevilled Victorian housing reformers. For whatever reason there was a political realization that the post-war generation would not tolerate previous living conditions. A Housing and Town Planning Act of 1919 designed to meet this changed situation was less than adequate; nevertheless, it set in train a sequence of legislation which was eventually to transform not only the appearance of Britain's towns but the whole framework of society.

In the inter-war period, the extension of suburbia was due mainly to the vast spread of residential estates. These were no longer catering simply for the middle classes who had the time and resources to commute. After the war many authorities developed policies of building low-density housing estates in the suburbs with subsidized rents for the working classes. In the 1930s this was complemented by private enterprise provision of cheap suburban homes. It was, however, the involvement of local authorities which constituted a 'minor revolution' in the standards of working class housing and living. In John Burnett's words:

> The local authorities' housing policies therefore institutionalised for the working classes the process of suburbanisation which the middle classes had followed since at least the middle of the nineteenth century, but developed what had been a largely unconscious process for the few into a planned policy for the many.[9]

This does not mean that local authorities became the main builders of housing, nor that they were only concerned with suburban estates. Private builders were still responsible for most new houses in the inter-war period; local authorities also had to deal with slum clearance and the housing of the working classes in city-centre tenements. What is important is that municipalities were now the agents of experimentation in working class housing, and as a result central government was increasingly involved as the controller of minimum standards and the arbiter of good practice. The Second World War encouraged and enhanced the planning and direction of housing. By 1950 significant advances had been made in the standards of housing particularly in relation to space, design and layout, and amenities and fittings. Higher standards had been brought within the reach of a much wider proportion of society. This did not however mean there was no longer a housing problem; there were still slums and sub-standard dwellings. What had changed was the basic level of expectation and scope of housing policy. Concern over the appearance of houses had by now been properly balanced by social considerations.

These architectural and social factors provided the context within which the model housing of the period developed and took effect. It had no reality outside that context. The model house at one and the same time affects the changing expectations of housing and the changing response of architects, designers and builders to the requirements of society. The significance and impact of model housing over the period 1851 to 1951, both in terms of housing reform and of the total housing stock, can only be assessed within this total picture. The identification and isolation of the model house presented here has another purpose; that is to concentrate on what people at particular points in time considered to be 'models' of design. These may represent either an ideal to be aimed at, or a considered response to existing conditions. With such an emphasis, the model house enables the identification of those factors which affect the design of housing and which influence its style, layout and facilities.

As such, model housing is a limited and very particular element in the housing market; it nevertheless provides a most useful tool for design historians and a productive vehicle for approaching the study of housing reform and improvement. At specific points of time it enables the examination of the origins of different attitudes and approaches to design, and allows consideration of how people over a period responded to economic conditions, how they sought to reflect changing attitudes and ideas in design patterns, how they incorporated technological developments and how they translated contemporary stylistic ideas and innovations into practical design possibilities for different social groups.

As a result, the model house during the period 1851 to 1951 is represented in a range of housing types – tenements, flats, rural cottages, bye-law terraces, municipal estates, suburban villas and bungalows. These resulted from a range of initiatives and interests. Many were brought forward by individual architects or designers, and presented as model schemes in the architectural press. In some cases they were commissioned by the building society or the organization involved in the reform of housing and the improvement of the conditions of the working class, or by an individual concerned for the better housing of his workforce or the exercise of benevolent philanthropy. In some cases model houses were the subject of competitions, which in turn might arise from enquiries, both public and private, into the state of housing and of domestic conditions for the working class in both town and country. These enquiries and reports were stimulated by particular events at particular times, such as the threats of cholera in the 1840s or of physical deterioration in the 1890s, or the pressure of heightened social awareness in war time, as occurred during both the First and Second World Wars.

Under these circumstances government, both national and local, emerged as a promoter of model housing, both in terms of disseminating information and laying down standards. The latter role had developed throughout the nineteenth century with the formulation of building regulations and the issuing of model bye-laws, indicating minimum acceptable standards of construction. This was taken a stage further in the twentieth century with the presentation of models for use by the public, and advice for both local authorities and private owners and builders as to how best to build and equip houses for the working class. Out of this arose a greater understanding of housing needs and a greater involvement on the part of the public. By the end of the period, the public were not only being consulted about what they considered a model home, but were also bringing forward their own ideas and practical suggestions. In this the model house was still filling its role as a means of instruction and as an educational force in society.

Through this means model housing was able to contribute to the reform of housing and the development of working class housing over the course of these 100 years in three main spheres. In the first place, it facilitated the transition of architectural ideas and innovations to the needs and requirements of ordinary housing. In the middle years of the nineteenth century the architectural profession made very little contribution to housing. Individual architects were not unaware of the situation, but in general the housing problem was not originally conceived of as an architectural problem. Architecture was seen as a matter of style to do with grand buildings and great houses, not a matter of organization to do with every-day needs. It was through the competitions and commissions for model housing which characterized the second half of the nineteenth century that architects, individually and later collectively, developed an interest in housing needs and began to bring contemporary notions of design and aesthetics to bear on this work. In the late nineteenth century, under the influence of architects like Webb and Voysey, there was a change from the conception of the house as a visual object to a view that good design must arise from the needs and requirements of the building. It was this attitude which produced in the twentieth century the idea of the 'house as a machine for living'. Through the model house in all its forms, architects were able to translate such ideas into practice.

At the same time, this functional concern was reflected in the attention given to the domestic comfort of the ordinary house. The model house was not just a matter of appearance, it was also about the quality of life within the house. On the one hand this was to do with the moral well-being of the inhabitants, and such concerns were upper-most in the minds of most early reformers. This was reflected in the attention given initially to the minimum number of bedrooms necessary to ensure the separation of the sexes and the sleeping arrangements for a working class family. It appeared in the debate over the parlour and the extent to which such facilities would serve to keep the menfolk at home and thereby away from the public house. Moral well-being, as well as physical well-being, underlay the arguments for low-density housing and the provision of individual gardens.

Such concern was, however, matched by that for the health and physical comfort of the poor. Model housing was a potent force in promoting improved sanitation and proper sewerage – the need not only for running water in each dwelling but also for the separation of essential services and activities within the home. In the twentieth century the increasing availability of low-cost heat and light from gas and electricity, broadened the scope of innovation. This, coupled with the abandonment of the idea that the standards of amenity should depend wholly and directly on the financial return from rent, meant that model housing served to raise expectations of domestic comfort and amenity, and to tackle the question of preferred solutions as distinct from simply minimal provision.

In these 100 years model housing had moved from a conception of housing as a social problem to the utilization of it as a means of social improvement. What did not change was the fact that in some form or other housing was used as a force for social control, and this was the third main contribution of model housing during this period. It was the emphasis and expectation that changed. In 1850 model housing was in practice reacting to the troubled decade of the 1840s and to the fear, on the one hand, that poor housing encouraged riot and revolution and, on the other, that poor housing led to poor health which in turn undermined the prosperity of the nation.

Such general concerns were reflected in the involvement of individual industrialists during the second half of the nineteenth century, when they built model housing for their workers with the explicit intention of improving their physical and moral well-being. Implicit in such actions however were the expectations of attracting a better quality workforce, of increasing their productivity and overall of enhancing management control over them. As Sidney Pollard has pointed out, workers' housing was a managerial problem, neglect of which could cause serious problems of factory discipline and shortage of labour. Model housing offered a direct means of social control. In town after town in the third quarter of the century model bye-laws were promulgated in response to urban unrest and radical pressure.

Nationally the arguments for more positive control of urban expansion and overcrowding of population were reinforced early in the twentieth century as a result of evidence of physical deterioration in some social classes. During the First World War housing became an urgent reconstruction issue because it related to so many other problems affecting both capitalism and working people. In these circumstances the models put forward went beyond a merely passive response to outside problems; in the way models were presented after the war they set out to ensure the survival of the status quo. As Swenarton has concluded, 'the design of the house was to prove to the people that revolution was unnecessary'. Between the wars local authorities' housing policies institutionalized for the working classes the process of sub-urbanization:

> What had been typical middle class characteristics – the privatisation of domestic life, cleanliness, sobriety, concern for the special needs of children – thereby became more widely diffused to a class whose rising standards of living and expectations encouraged the adoption of such values.[10]

Such expectations were reinforced during the Second World War and encouraged in its immediate aftermath. Throughout this process, however, model housing imparted to working class housing external values. It reflected a scaled-down version of middle class housing ideals. In this sense the model house was a practical means of encouraging the dominant values of society and of extending the process of social control. The history of that process reflects the changing attitudes to social problems and organization over a century from 1851 to 1951. In combination with those factors affecting the design of housing and affecting the standards of accommodation, these changing attitudes and changing requirements are illustrated in the model housing promoted at particular points during the course of these hundred years.

NOTES

1. Darley, G. (1975) *Villages of Vision*, London: Architectural Press, p. 8.

2. Knight, R.P. (1805) *An Analytical Inquiry into the Principles of Taste*. London; Price, U. (1794) *Essay on the Picturesque*.

3. Howitt, W. (1844) *The Rural Life of England*, 3rd ed. London, p. 412.

4. Eden, F.M. (1797) *The State of the Poor*, 3 vols. London; Kent, N. (1775) *Hints to Gentlemen of Landed Property*. London.

5. Muthesius, H. (1904/05) *Das Englische Haus*. Berlin (English edition: Sharp, D. (ed.) (1979) *The English House*. London: Crosby Lockwood Staples).

6. 38 & 39 Vic., c. 55.

7. 53 & 54 Vic., c. 70.

8. 8 Edw. VII, c. 44.

9. Burnett, J. (1978) *A Social History of Housing 1815–1970*. Newton Abbot: David and Charles.

10. *Ibid.*, p. 309.

SECTION II

Case Studies

The Prince Consort's Model Houses in the Great Exhibition of 1851

The model houses at the Great Exhibition of 1851 belonged to the Prince Consort, and it was because of his personal interest in their construction that permission was granted to place them on the ground of the Cavalry Barracks opposite the Exhibition. Though this venture is always associated with its royal patron, the design represents very much the latest ideas in dwellings for the labouring classes as expounded by the architect Henry Roberts. He was also responsible for the design of the first cottages promoted for twenty families by the Windsor Royal Society under the patronage of the Queen and Prince Albert. As with the cottages at the Great Exhibition, these were put forward with the object of demonstrating that good housing could be supplied at a price which would give a modest return on capital.

Roberts had been appointed honorary architect to the Society for Improving the Condition of the Labouring Classes and as such had addressed the Royal Institute of British Architects in 1850 on the subject of the dwellings of the labouring classes, with a view to encouraging the profession's involvement in the design of dwellings which would conduce to the comfort, and promote the health and good morals of the labouring classes:

> It is only the merest fraction of the working classes who have it directly within their own power in any way to help themselves, as respects their dwellings. Hence the greater claim for the kind consideration of those whose position and circumstances give them the opportunity of providing in this respect for their wants, on the sound principle of receiving in return a fair percentage on the necessary outlay of capital.

In sympathy with these ideas, the Prince supported the project for erecting, in conjunction with the Great Exhibition, a set of houses which would serve as a model for those concerned to diffuse more widely the benefits of healthy dwellings amongst the labouring people and thereby assist their physical and moral improvement. As well as his theoretical interest in the subject and his active promotion of the housing needs of the labouring classes, Roberts had also gained practical experience of the problem of building model dwellings in towns. As architect to the Society for Improving the Condition of the Labouring Classes, he had been responsible for the Model Dwellings in Streatham Street, which as Tarn has recorded, 'set a standard of accommodation which was well in advance of contemporary practice, and perhaps because the standard was lavish in relation to the rents which the poor could pay, the building was not very profitable'.

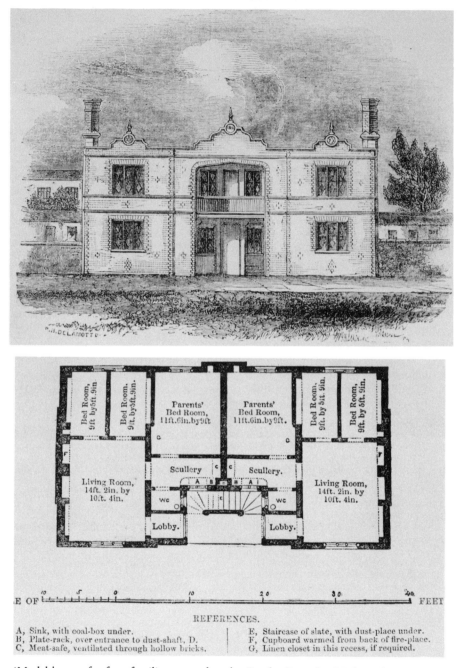

A, Sink, with coal-box under.
B, Plate-rack, over entrance to dust-shaft, D.
C, Meat-safe, ventilated through hollow bricks.

E, Staircase of slate, with dust-place under.
F, Cupboard warmed from back of fire-place.
G, Linen closet in this recess, if required.

'Model houses for four families, erected at the Cavalry Barracks, Hyde Park, in connection with the Exposition of the Works of Industry of All Nations, 1851, by His Royal Highness Prince Albert, KG.'

There he introduced the system of open staircases, with extended galleries, to give access to the upper-floor tenements of houses occupied by a number of families. This system was reproduced in the Exhibition model houses on the grounds that it afforded advantages in rendering the tenements completely distinct, prevented the communication of infectious disease and entitled the dwellings to exemption from the House Tax. As such the model was presented by Roberts for 'architects and others who have not studied this subject much' and who, he felt, might find it of service in meeting the needs of working people in thickly populated towns, 'where the cost of land usually renders it impossible to provide them with self-contained houses'.

The principles underlying these model dwellings were therefore of general applicability. In the first place Roberts argued that in order to be healthy even the most humble abode must be dry and well ventilated. This required attention to be given to the situation, foundations, and drainage, and secondly to the construction material of the external walls and roofs. To secure ventilation, there had to be a free circulation of air secured through a sufficient number and size of openings, along with adequate height of the rooms – at least 7 ft 6 in and preferably 9 ft in towns. It was recognized that the number and area of the apartments needed to be in proportion to the probable number of occupants; however as a general rule in family houses there should be not fewer than three sleeping apartments, each with distinct and independent access in order to secure due separation of the sexes. Roberts considered that the living room should be not less than 140 ft^2, and that the parents' bedroom should likewise be of a minimum size of 100 ft^2. In the main bedroom there should be a fireplace in case of sickness, and in every room, especially those bedrooms with no fireplaces, there should be an opening for the escape of vitiated air; this could be secured through on opening near the ceiling or through a flue built into the wall. Some such satisfactory system of ventilation was thought essential. For this purpose he drew attention to a wide range of patent ventilating bricks, perforated glass and sliding screens.

In addition to these very practical points, Roberts believed that for the comfort and health of the inmates of every tenement, the protection afforded by an internal lobby or closed porch was of importance, as was the relative position of doors and fireplaces in the living-room, which should be so arranged that 'there may be at least one snug corner free from draught'. Casement windows should be made to open outwards, because of the great difficulty found in rendering them weather tight in the lower class of buildings. Hollow bricks and tile arches in the construction of floors improved the insulation of buildings, it was recommended. Finally, if model dwellings were to attract tenants then they must also attract sunlight and avoid a gloomy appearance.

Roberts applied these principles to the model houses built for Prince Albert and he described them accordingly in the catalogue for the Great Exhibition:

> In its general arrangement, the building is adapted for the occupation of four families of the class of manufacturing and mechanical operatives, who usually reside in towns or their immediate vicinity; and as the value of land, which leads to the economising of

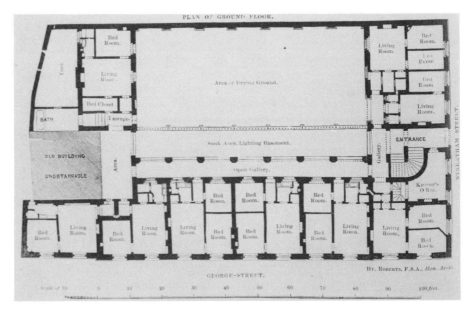

Model houses for families in Streatham Street, Bloomsbury.

space, by the placing of more than one family under the same roof, in some cases, renders the addition of a third and even fourth storey desirable, the plan has been suited to such an arrangement, without any other alteration than the required increase in the strength of the walls. The most prominent peculiarity of the design is that of the receding and protected central open staircase, with the connecting gallery on the first floor, formed of slate and sheltered from the weather by the construction of the main roof, which also screens the entrances to the dwellings. . . . The four tenements are arranged on precisely the same plan, two on each floor.

Each was an independent unit, with its own scullery, closet, water supply, fireplace and dust shaft. This was the ideal of the Society, and within the internal space available Roberts carefully planned for a living room and scullery with three bedrooms opening off these. This allowed a separate bedroom for the children of each sex and for the parents, and provided rooms of reasonable shape and each with a window and proper ventilation. Apart from the accommodation, the 'pecularities' of the building lay in its exclusive use of hollow bricks for the walls and partitions, and the entire absence of timber in the floors and roof. The latter were formed of flat arches of hollow brickwork, set in cement and tied by wrought iron rods. It was claimed that the building was thus rendered fire-proof and much less liable to decay than those of ordinary construction. It was established that the cost of the four houses built on the plan of this model structure would be between £440 and £480.

As practical examples of what could be economically achieved through careful planning and attention to detail, these cottages established the model house as a means of instruction and encouragement. Of their effectiveness Roberts was to write:

> Amongst the number of visitors to the Prince's model houses, amounting to upwards of 250,000, many gave evidence of their having duly appreciated the object for which they were placed in the Exhibition, viz, the conveying of practical information, calculated to promote the much needed improvement of the dwellings of the working classes, and also stimulating those whose position and circumstances enabled them to carry out similar undertakings and thus, without pecuniary sacrifice, permanently to benefit those who are greatly dependent on others for their home and family comforts . . . Scarcely any foreigners who visited the Exhibition of 1851 returned without examining the Prince's model houses, and but few left without carrying back to their several countries some of the publications bearing on the improvement of the dwellings of the labouring classes which were abundantly distributed. My own opportunities of judging the effect of this little structure enabled me to say that it gave to the movement an impulse such as it has not received from any other single effort, the results of which have spread far and wide.

SOURCES

Roberts, H. (1850) *The Improvement of the Dwellings of the Labouring Classes*. London.

Roberts, H. (1851) *The Model Houses for Families*. London.

Roberts, H. (1862) *Essentials of a Healthy Dwelling*. London.

Society for Improving the Condition of the Labouring Classes (1851) *Plans and Descriptions of Model Dwellings*. London.

Model Dwellings for Agricultural Labourers, 1850

THE attention of landed proprietors has often been directed to the necessity for the improvement of labourers' cottages, and in not a few instances the entire aspect of a village and neighbourhood has in this respect been completely changed by the well directed efforts of a single landlord.

In 1850 the Duke of Bedford, who was then engaged in re-building over 400 decayed properties on his estates, wrote to the Royal Agricultural Society, which was much exercised by the problems affecting the housing of the labouring classes, on the principles which should promote the involvement of the nobility and landed gentry in the provision of dwellings:

> To improve the dwellings of the labouring class, and afford them the means of greater cleanliness, health, and comfort in their own homes; to extend education, and thus raise the social and moral habits of those most valuable members of the community, are amongst the first duties, and ought to be amongst the truest pleasures, of every landlord . . . I shall not dwell, as I might, on the undeniable advantages of making the rural population contented with their condition, and of promoting that mutual good-will between the landed proprietor and the tenants and labourers on his estate, which sound policy and the higher motives of humanity alike recommend.

The designing of improved dwellings for agricultural labourers, arranged on the most economical plan, with proper regard to the health and comfort of the occupants, had repeatedly been made the subject of architectural competitions in the 1840s. Many of the results were quite unsatisfactory as models, and in 1850 the Society for Improving the Condition of the Labouring Classes collected together examples of good practice by various landlords, including the Bedford estate, and published these in order '. . . to facilitate the adoption of plans which combine in their arrangement every point essential to the health, comfort, and moral habits of the labourer and his family, with that due regard to stability and economy of construction, which is essential to their general usefulness . . .'.

These plans displayed considerable variety, not only in the number and disposition of the rooms, but also in their external elevations. This was intended both to meet the needs of different sizes of families and to allow for diversity in the grouping of cottages together. On the grounds of economy, however, most of the dwellings were designed in pairs, with care being taken to prevent, as far as possible, the interference of adjoining families with each other, by placing the entrance doors at the opposite extremities of the cottages. At the same time, economy was achieved by carrying up the chimney stack in the centre in order to obtain the greatest amount of warmth from the flues.

Each dwelling consists of a living-room, the general superficial dimensions of which are about 150 ft. clear of the chimney projection. A scullery, containing not less than about 60 ft. or 70 ft. superficial, which is of sufficient size for ordinary domestic purposes. without offering a temptation to its use as a living-room for the family; besides a copper, and in some cases a brick oven, provision is made for a fireplace in all the sculleries, by which arrangement the necessity for a fire in the living-room through the summer is avoided. A pantry for food, a closet in the living-room, and a fuel store out of the scullery are provided in all the cottages.

The sleeping apartments, in conformity with the principle of separating the sexes, so essential to morality and decency, are generally three in number each having its distinct access; their dimensions somewhat vary – the parents' bedroom in no instance contains less than about 100 ft. superficial, whilst the smaller rooms for the children average from 70 ft. to 80 ft. superficial. The height from the ground floor to the first floor is 8 ft. 9 in., giving nearly 8 ft. clear height for the living-room. The bedrooms are 7 ft. 9 in. where ceiled to the collar pieces and 4 ft. to the top of the wall-plate, which, for the security of the roof, is in no case severed by the dormer windows.

These designs generally provided for three bedrooms, but it was recognized that there were circumstances in which a smaller number would be satisfactory. There was always the danger that a 'spare bedroom' would be used for a lodger. If this were to be allowed then it was argued that the sleeping arrangements for the family should be entirely separate from those for the lodger, and there was a plan providing for this on the ground floor of the dwelling. No costs were given for erecting these cottages as it was considered that these would vary considerably between different localities, depending on the availability of materials. What was provided was detailed practical advice on the best ways of constructing model dwellings.

In reference to situation, where it is practicable the front should have somewhat of a southern aspect; the embosoming in trees should be avoided, and particular attention ought to be paid to secure a dry foundation; where this is not otherwise obtainable, artificial means should be adopted by forming a substrata of concrete about 12 in. thick, or by bedding slate in cement, or laying asphalt through the whole thickness of the wall under the floor level. The vicinity of good water and proper drainage are points of obvious importance. A gravelly soil is always preferable to clay, and a low situation is seldom healthy.

It is desirable that every cottage should stand in its own enclosed garden of not less than about ⅛ of an acre, and have a separate entrance from the public road. One well may generally be made to answer for two or more cottages, and it is of great importance that it be so placed as not to be liable to contamination . . .

Detailed information was also incorporated with regard to materials to be used and the standards to be applied in model labourers' cottages. Thus while brick was the

DOUBLE COTTAGES FOR AGRICULTURAL DISTRICTS. No. 6.

FRONT ELEVATION.

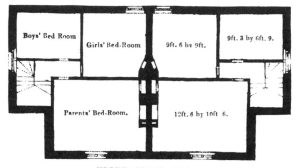

Boys' Bed Room

Girls' Bed-Room

9ft. 6 by 9ft.

9ft. 3 by 6ft. 9.

Parents' Bed-Room.

12ft. 6 by 10ft. 6.

UPPER FLOOR PLAN.

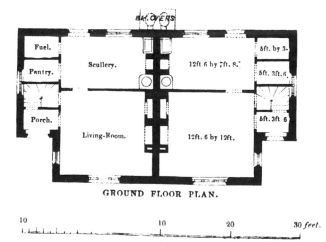

BK. OVENS

Fuel.

Pantry.

Scullery.

12ft 6 by 7ft. 8.

5ft. by 3.

5ft. 3ft. 6.

Porch.

5ft. 3ft 6

Living-Room.

12ft. 6 by 12ft.

GROUND FLOOR PLAN.

10   10   20   30 feet.

DOUBLE COTTAGES FOR AGRICULTURAL DISTRICTS. No. 1.

FRONT ELEVATION.

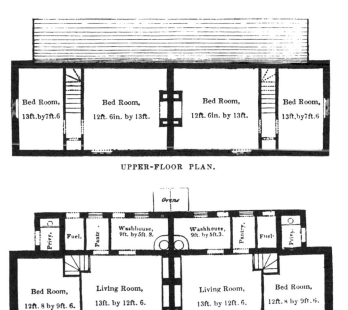

UPPER-FLOOR PLAN.

GROUND-FLOOR PLAN.

Scale of

Above and left: Examples from the Society for Improving the Condition of the Labouring Classes, *Plans and Suggestions for Dwellings*.

normal building material, specifications were given for the use of other substances. The value of hollow bricks as a means of preventing dampness and of lowering the cost of internal walls and partitions was advocated; the efficiency of other patented building materials, such as concrete and artificial stone, was assessed. Landlords were advised that the ground floors of cottages should be ventilated by means of air bricks and roofs constructed of tiles rather than slates, as being more economical and better insulators. In some of the examples the walls of the living-room were left unplastered, but this was not recommended as it resulted in very little saving and the brickwork then required additional care. All other rooms downstairs, however, were left unplastered and in these annual whitewashing at the expense of the tenants, was advocated. Finally arrangements were proposed for the ventilation of closets, and where possible for the provision of water from a pump.

These practical details relating to the construction and equipment of model dwellings were positively linked to the use tenants made of their cottages and the role of model dwellings in improving the quality of life. Such considerations were catered for in the advice given on the management of cottages, and were illustrated through a model agreement for the letting of cottages. This included the following controlling clauses:

1. Only one family will be permitted to reside in a cottage, and the tenant is not to underlet or take in a lodger, or carry on any trade or business therein, or keep poultry or a pig without leave first obtained in writing from the landlord or his agent.

2. The windows are to be kept clean, and the ground floor chimneys to be swept once in six months. No alteration – by fixing or removing shelves or other fixtures – is to be made without permission of the landlord or his agent.

3. The windows, ovens, and coppers, are to be kept in repair by the landlord, and the cost of such repairs to be re-paid by the tenant; as well as the cost of whitewashing once a year, with the making good of any damaged plastering.

4. The fences to be kept in repair by the landlord, and the cost of the repairs to be re-paid in equal proportions, by the tenants of the cottages enclosed within such fence.

5. The tenant to clear away the ashes, and to remove all manure, etc, which may have been laid near the cottage every week.

6. The gardens in front of the cottages to be kept in good order, and the cottages themselves in a neat and tidy state to the satisfaction of the landlord or his agent.

As many working-class families were to discover over the next 100 years, model dwellings had their disadvantages. Not only did they involve restrictions on tenants' freedom, but they also involved considerable intervention on the part of the landlord. From the outset dwellings were seen as being a means of both improvement and instruction for their inhabitants.

SOURCES

Hartshorne, C.H. (1850) *The System of Building Cottages pursued on the Estate of his Grace the Duke of Bedford*. Northampton.

Journal of the Royal Agricultural Society, 1850.

Roberts, H (1850) *The Dwellings of the Labouring Classes, their Arrangement and Construction*. London.

Society for Improving the Condition of the Labouring Classes (1851) *Plans and Suggestions for Dwellings*. London.

Case Study Three

The Model Dwellings of High Victorian Philanthropy, 1863

Henry Darbishire, the architect of the Peabody Trust established in 1862, published a paper in 1863 on 'Dwellings for the Poor'. This established the principles and standards underlying the design of the early Peabody Estates, which in turn influenced the work of other housing companies during the 1860s and 1870s.

Darbishire had two main concerns: one was to build cheaply; the other was to build appropriate dwellings for working class habits and lifestyles, as he perceived them. Question of cost was in part determined by the Trust, which sought a modest return from its housing developments – the classic policy of 'philanthropy at five-per-cent'. At the same time, there had been considerable criticism of earlier model dwellings in London on account of their cost and their consequent inability to cater for the poorest classes. It was argued that high standards of accommodation were a mistake and that there would have to be a reduction in housing standards. Model dwellings were for the first time associated with minimum dwellings, which in any case, it was claimed, would be more in keeping with the interests of the poor. 'Lavish facilities' would be wasted on those who did not know how to use them and who preferred their own arrangements.

These two issues of costs and standards were closely related, if the housing problem was to be dealt with in a commercial way. The latter however was also a social question of whether model dwellings with improved amenities and facilities should be a means of effecting an improvement in the poor themselves. By the 1860s the prevalent view was that the system did not improve the people and that a better environment alone would not solve the social problems of the time.

Darbishire therefore started from the premise that improved buildings would be more popular the closer they approximated to their 'miserable predecessors' in both appearance and character. The problem was how to design new homes for the poor which incorporated such improvements as would lead to the 'gradual abandonment of injurious habits', but would not affront domestic prejudices. To do this meant building to meet the 'requirements and peculiarities' of the inhabitants of the districts concerned. However beautiful the dwelling, Darbishire believed it would be ineffective, if the tenant did not feel himself at home.

> If there is anything in the world that a poor man hates or a poor man's children are educated to hate with cordial, sincere, and unquenchable hatred, it is fresh air. No preaching, reasoning, expostulation, or cajolement will induce him to breathe freely among his own Penates, if he can help it . . . No one will deny that dwellings must be

ventilated, but few will be able to say how it is to be done. Beyond supplying doors that do not fit too close, windows that will open at the top and bottom, and fireplaces with air channels underneath the floor, it is extremely difficult to know how to proceed further without detection. A ventilator, once discovered instantly becomes useless. It is pasted over if small, and if large is made the receptacle of every cast-off garment, from a bonnet to an old shoe. The most successful ventilators that I have tried are some perforated bricks, so adapted that they will admit the external air, without causing a draft . . . and the air is so diffused by its passage through the narrow channels with which the bricks are provided that the paste brush is seldom considered necessary.

Closely aligned to the subject of ventilation was that of drainage:

. . . after the foundations, no portion of a building deserves more attention than its drains. In dwellings provided for persons who are not remarkable for the care they bestow on the property of others, it is especially desirable that the drain-pipes should be of the best description, and that their diameter should be larger than those employed under ordinary circumstances, because their liabilities to obstruction are very much greater. Boots, brushes, bones and pieces of old furniture, and even pieces of old clothes, are not unfrequently found in the drains of poor neighbourhoods. That these and similarly unwelcoming intruders may be easily removed, it is desirable that the main drains should be external to the building; that they should be supplied with examination holes at certain intervals for the purposes of repair and cleansing; and that they should possess the means of being regularly flushed with water. None but the inferior drains should be laid within the building, and these should take the shortest possible course to the main drains.

When Darbishire turned his attention to the construction of the model dwelling and the materials to be used inside it, he came up against man (or at least, presumably, the working man and his family) as a 'destructive animal'. All surfaces had to be resilient to every possible onslaught. Thus with regard to the floors:

Wood is certainly not very hard; it is inviting for nails; is apt to get dirty and probably difficult to clean, and yet, in my opinion, a wood floor is the best that can be constructed for our purpose. If it be not very hard, it is not very rigid, and its elasticity enables it to bear heavy and sudden blows without injury. If firewood or coal be broken up on any other floor than a wooden one, the concussion is much more injurious. If nails are driven into the joints or the boards themselves, they are easily extracted, and leave no mark behind them; and if an extra amount of scrubbing is necessary to keep them clean, no-one will deny that visible cleanliness is better than hidden dirt. Tile and asphalt floors have often been recommended as the best; but though the floor might have a clean appearance they are cold to the feet when uncovered by a carpet; they are more liable to injury than floorboards, and they are more troublesome to repair and to replace when defective.

The choice of construction materials and surface coverings was not just to do with the question of durability but was closely aligned to the question of cleanliness, and thereby inevitably moral improvement:

Peabody Dwellings in Blackfrairs, designed by Henry Darbishire.

The working man is a nomad, as much so as the Arab of the desert. The nature of his employment compels him to wander from place to place like an unquiet spirit. He cannot, therefore, be regarded under any circumstances, as a permanent tenant; and, as the improvement of his habits and tastes is one of the objects most desired by those who undertake to improve his home, it is of importance that, when he first takes possession of it, he should find it clean and fit for immediate use. Now if dirty walls are to be re-papered every time a new tenant objects to their appearance, it is evident that much time and money must be most profitlessly consumed; whereas, if the walls are merely coloured, a couple of hours and a pail full of colour suffice to restore them to their original freshness.

This preference for painted brick as against plaster or wallpaper was further motivated by the belief that the working man was bound to carry infestation into his home and plaster and paper provided a home for insects and vermin. Painted walls could be more easily cleansed and disinfected, and as Darbishire pointed out there was no reason why they should not provide an atmosphere of cheeriness and comfort at the same time.

The habits of cleanliness were to be further encouraged with the attachment of a laundry to each block of model dwellings, which should be equipped in an effective and practical manner:

In my opinion it is important that the accommodation should be as simple as possible, that the supply of water should be near at hand, and that all artificial means of drying, excepting, of course, clothes-wringers should be avoided . . . There should be a ten-gallon copper, furnished with a cold water service and tin ladel . . . It is desirable that the cistern, or source from which the water supply is obtained, should be as close to the laundry as possible, in order that the piping may be short, require few joints and bends, and be free from the risks which attend a variety of levels . . . The artificial means of drying clothes, which are adopted with advantage in the public washouses, are to be avoided in small laundries, because they require fuel, machinery, and supervision, which cannot be supplied and maintained without considerable expense, and which do not secure advantages at all commensurate with their attendant risk and cost. As far as my experience teaches, I find that clothes are easily and effectively dried if they are protected from rain and suspended in strong cross currents of air, and that, wherever spaces suitable for this purpose can be obtained, other expedients are not required.

In all, this was a severely practical model, and one which involved a very low opinion of working class interests and expectations. It is not surprising then that with regard to the blocks in general, Darbishire advised against the temptation to build picturesquely and to try experiments. Projections and angles were to be avoided in favour of straight lines. The blocks were to rely on good proportions for their appearance rather than variety in design or the addition of ornamentation.

The result was a series of developments in the 1860s for the Peabody Trust in London. The sites were densely developed with rectangular blocks which were laid out round a central open space which served as a playground and forecourt. The

Peabody Buildings, Herbrand Street Estate.

Peabody Estate, Turpentine Lane, Pimlico.

blocks were generally four or five storeys high and had central staircases serving corridor access systems. They were severe and unadorned, and demonstrated all the qualities which earned them the name of 'barrack blocks'. In Tarn's words, 'They seem today memorable for their grimness and physical bulk; a new and depressing characteristic had been added to the model housing movement'.

This was reinforced by the internal economy of the buildings with 'associated' flats sharing common lavatories and sculleries. These model dwellings established basic standards of accommodation, construction and sanitation. Darbishire did not believe that the habits and behaviour of the poor would necessarily be improved by their removal to enhanced environments. In any case, the process would be slow and would have to be taken stage by stage. His solution therefore combined social realism with practical economy.

SOURCES

Darbishire, H.A. (1863) Dwellings for the poor. *Building News*, **X**.

Tarn, J.N. (1973) *Five Per Cent Philanthropy: An Account of Housing in Urban Areas between 1840 and 1914*. London: Cambridge University Press.

Akroyden

It was the conjunction of the building society tradition in the Pennine towns with the dynamic of the mill owner that produced one of the most interesting experiments in housing reform and community planning in the nineteenth century. Edward Akroyd's settlement at Akroyden is well known; but it was only the first of a series of similarly motivated experiments in the area during the 1860s. The term 'model village' is used here in a special sense, since these settlements represent a conscious effort to overcome the weaknesses of the ordinary building society – failure to improve the design of working class houses, failure to deal with the overall character of an estate, and failure to meet the needs of the majority of working class men. Akroyd, in his scheme, primarily sought to secure '. . . a uniformity of style and a protection against the depreciation which the purchaser of a good house often sustains by the juxtaposition of an inferior building'.

To this end, Akroyd worked in conjuction with a building society – the Akroyden Building Association – founded in 1860 and capitalized by the Halifax Permanent Benefit Building Society. As the promoter he made himself responsible for the layout of the site and the provision of adequate drainage. But his 'chief and primary object' was the erection of a better class of workmen's cottages than could be secured through the ordinary channels of building speculation; such cottages being designed by an architect, subject to the approval of a committee of the Building Association. A clerk of works was employed to look after the contractors and to see that the work was properly executed.

> These are especially the points on which a working man wants help, because he can understand little of architects' plans and designs; and whatever knowledge he may have of the contractor's work, his influence and control will be very slight.

The second way in which Akroyd sought to improve on the normal building society was by enlarging its scope, and to this end he gave assistance in raising the £40 deposit or one-quarter of the purchase money. For as he wrote, 'This sum may be as far out of the reach of the members as the whole amount for which he subscribes.' Therefore, Akroyd, as promoter, guaranteed the deposit and the Association, with such security, was willing to forego prepayment and simply increase the scale of weekly payments.

During the earlier years of the nineteenth century many industrialists were involved in promoting some form of building society activity among their workers. The great advance made by Akroyd, however, was that he combined the financial inducements with an attempt at architectural distinction. His influence on the

Akroyden: Elevation of cottages facing the green.

housing reform movement stemmed from his effort to impart to a self-help organization concepts of planning and design that traditionally went with the model village of the industrialist. For the scheme at Akroyden, Akroyd commissioned the architect George Gilbert Scott to prepare plans and designs in the domestic Gothic – a style which he felt '. . . pleases the fancy, strengthens house and home attachment, entwines the present with the memory of the past, and promises, in spite of opposition and prejudice, to become the national style of modern, as it was of old England'.

This was a view that was not, however, shared by the original members of the Building Association who, although they liked the look of it, considered it antiquated, inconvenient, wanting in light and not adapted to modern requirements. The dormer windows, which they claimed reminded them of almshouses and were thus degrading, they forced the designer to remove. The actual houses were built of stone and arranged in blocks of nine in a double row around an open square. None of the houses had any garden, only a backyard containing an ash place and privy – allotments were provided close by. The noticeable feature of the scheme is its density – planned originally with 350 houses for the 14-acre site. Scott's scheme was modified by the local architect, W.H. Crossland, who supervised the work, so that the whole of the central area was covered with terraces.

The first houses erected in 1861 had a living room, kitchen and two bedrooms, and cost £130. But in the second block of twelve erected the following year, the members requested that a parlour be included. *The Builder* felt that more gifted workmen were often driven from their homes to places of less profitable resort through the want of a

Opposite: Akroyden: General layout and plans of cottages.

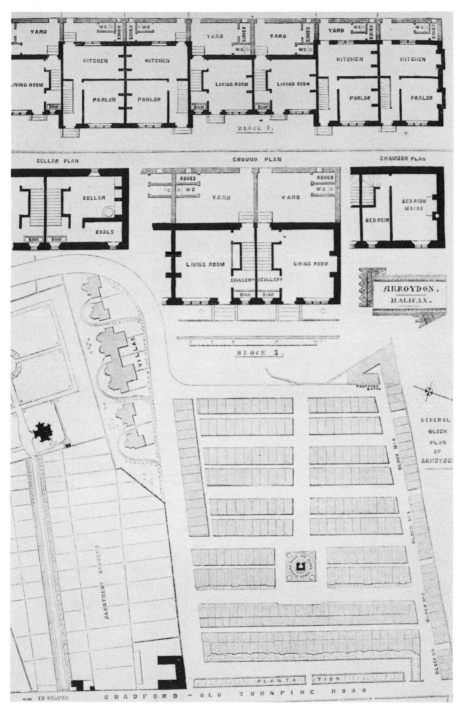

quiet room in their own homes, and it therefore supported the provision of a parlour, though acknowledging the danger that such a room might be kept for Sunday use only. In this block there were two houses costing £300 each, six at £210 and four at £150. In later blocks there were houses costing as much as £460. By 1886 the fifty-nine houses in Salisbury and York Terraces were valued at between £8 and £12 per annum, the four houses in Chester Road at £18 and the Akroyden villas at £42 10s.

Such houses were obviously not aimed at a wholly working class population. Indeed Akroyd was not trying to create a one class community. As *The Builder* noted: 'He is desirous of keeping up the old English notion of a village – the squire, as head and centre of all progress, then the tenant farmers and lastly the working population'.

Likewise, Akroyden was not simply an owner-occupier development. Akroyd remained the land owner, and though he was willing to sustain a loss on the first blocks, by subsidizing the original proprietors so as to secure the erection of houses according to his own designs, he felt this was necessary because ' . . . the working classes were so little accustomed to a really good house of pleasing elevation and were unwilling to pay the cost'. But he believed that the houses would obtain an adequate rental to protect him from material loss in the future, and yet would insure to the proprietor or member a good return for his outlay. On the £130 house he calculated that the proprietor could expect a 6 per cent return. It was reckoned that property investment at Akroyden was more secure in that the purchaser was protected against the depreciation of his own property by the juxtaposition of an inferior building. This was the self-help model which would enable the successful artisan to raise himself by his own action. Through the model house came moral and pecuniary benefits.

It was felt that by such schemes, not only did part of the working class benefit financially but that they thereby gradually raised the standard of all working class housing. From his own experience, Akroyd was convinced that: 'If the attempt bring no profit, or even occasion pecuniary loss, in no other way can the said benefits be conferred upon working men at so slight a loss – benefits which entail no degradation and wound no self-respect, but, on the contrary, confer independence, whilst the achievement of that independence constitutes a *habit* of saving, most useful in after life'.

SOURCES

Akroyd, E. (1862) *On Improved Dwellings for the Working Classes*. London.

Bretton, R. (1948) Colonel Edward Akroyd. *Halifax Antiquarian Society Transactions*.

The Builder, **XXI**, 1863.

Hole, J. (1866) *The Homes of the Working Classes, with Suggestions for their Improvement*. London.

Holyoake, G.J. (1866) *The History of Co-operation in Halifax and of some other Institutions around it*. London.

Transactions of the National Association for the Promotion of Social Science, 1862.

The Architecture of Labourers' Cottages, 1862

> It would be a waste of time, yet almost amusing, to run over the marvellous mistakes which have been made in prize cottages, even by our leading societies. Some of the very worst models which I know have been ushered into the world as model designs. Some without any pantry – one with an ornamental verandah over the scullery – another with separate chimney shaft to nearly every grate – another with classical pediment to the gable, and Gothic moulded battlements to the pig sty. I pass over the outrageous bargeboards and extravagant hipknots and other absurdities, added with the idea of giving an architectural character, and some quite impracticable . . .

Since the first flush of enthusiasm for the Picturesque had died down, the work of various landlords and bodies interested in cottage building had begun to take effect. From the 1840s new building and architectural journals had published model plans and analyses of the requirements of rural accommodation, and numerous new pattern books for such cottages had appeared. Nevertheless the problem remained. The activity of the previous decade established two characteristics of the model dwellings movement: firstly, that the production of plans and even the building of model dwellings does not of itself provide a solution; secondly, many so-called models were not necessarily improvements and were certainly not always realistic alternatives.

By the 1860s both reformers and improving landlords were increasingly aware of these limitations and were addressing themselves to the very practical problems that they posed.

Such was the background to the lecture on the subject of 'Labourers' Cottages and their bearing upon Architecture' given by Rev. Thomas James to the Architectural Museum, which had been established within the South Kensington Museum as an early centre of architectural education. He based this lecture on the extensive work of C.W. Strickland for the Yorkshire Agricultural Society.

Not only had the situation with regard to labourers' dwellings not improved since 1850, it had in fact deteriorated with the continuing distinction between closed and open parishes, and the concentration of estates into fewer hands. Until 1865 poor rates were levied on house property and this meant that it was in the interests of land-owners to demolish any accommodation not absolutely necessary for their needs. The corollary of this was the continuing influx of population into those open parishes which resulted in further overcrowding, with its associated problems. The result was a housing situation which behind its picturesque exterior was deteriorating, with damp broken-down hovels, without windows and proper roofs, and with inadequate

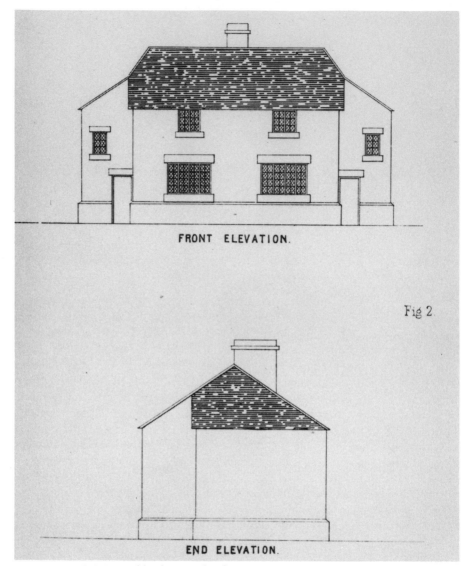

FRONT ELEVATION.

Fig 2.

END ELEVATION.

C.W. Strickland: example of cottage construction and design.

accommodation for the number of inhabitants. Despite some landowners' efforts to provide improved cottages, the mass of property reflected a 'hideous picture':

> The picture of rural housing in the 1860s was, then, a patchwork of good, bad and terrible, crumbling mud and thatched survivals from an earlier age interspersed here and there with tidy new brick and tile cottages on model estates, heightening the contrast between 'closed' and 'open' parishes . . . The problem was not seen as a national one so much as a local, individual and moral one.

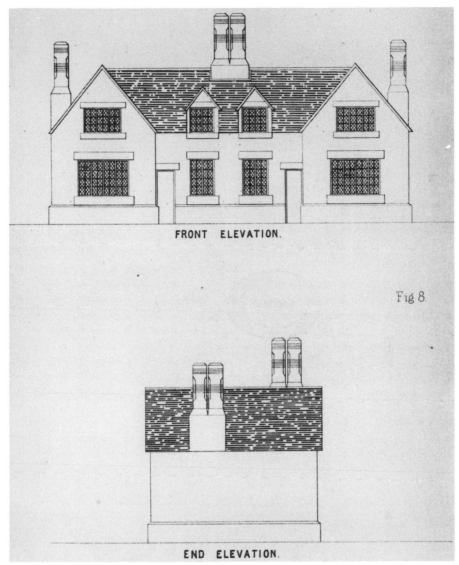

FRONT ELEVATION.

Fig 8.

END ELEVATION.

C.W. Strickland: example of cottage construction and design.

With regard to those model cottages which had been built, these had been subject to certain standard controls, as the Enclosure Commissioners since 1845 had been able to loan public money for estate improvements and in doing so had enforced minimum standards. They had refused to approve the use of poor bricks or unseasoned timbers; they had insisted on the provision of adequate sanitary arrangements and sufficient sleeping space. They were 'willing to adopt any plans which afforded a reasonable amount of accommodation and provided for the separation of

the sexes, and for health and comfort and decency'. In the matter of style, they
allowed builders freedom to indulge their own tastes and fancies, as long as these
could be contained within the limits of cost efficiency and reasonable living
standards.

It was therefore to this question of style and appearance that the Rev. James
addressed himself:

> While the difficulty of attaining good street architecture seems, judging from its
> rarity, almost insuperable, everybody supposes that he could build a cottage . . . but,
> of the thousand cottage plans that have been designed for the country labourer, there
> are scarcely more than three or four which he really likes, or would care to live in. It is
> notorious that the old mud hovels of the past, the concretion of many generations, had
> far more comforts and charms for the peasant, than most of the new spick and span new
> model cottages, premiated at the last agricultural show.

James was concerned that established architects did not condescend to tackle the
problem of cottage architecture, and he stressed that the style of development must
arise from the simple elements of cottage building:

> . . . effect should be obtained not by straining to produce it, but by carrying out in
> good proportion, and combining in due harmony, what is essentially requisite for the
> convenience of the house; how entirely all shams and concealed constructions are to be

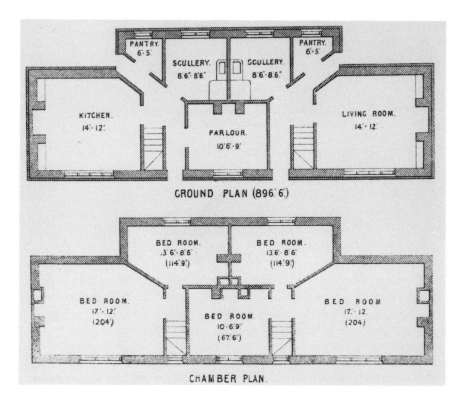

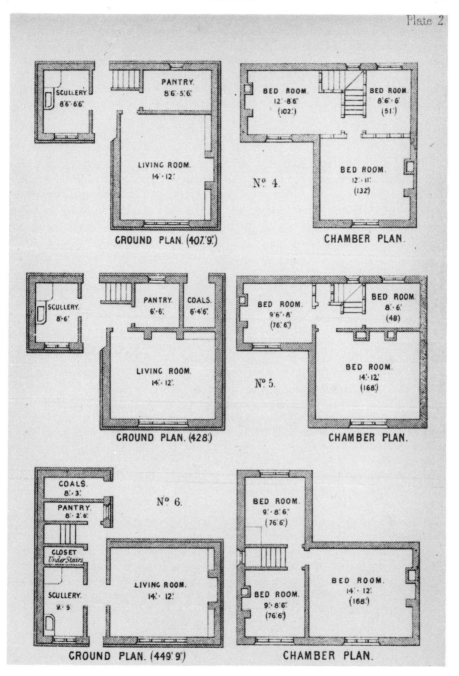

Plate 2.

Above and opposite: C.W. Strickland: model plans for labourers' cottages.

eschewed, how the interior wants of the house must give the character to the outward elevation, and not a preconceived elevation warp the interior arrangements to its lines. I am convinced that, of all the so-called picturesque cottages built during this century, the external view was drawn before the ground plan was designed – indeed, fifty years ago, I think that this must have been the professional practice with regard to all classes of building. Even now, I fear, the picturesque idea of what is wanted for a certain site floats through the mind, before the prosaic wants of the future occupier are listened to.

James therefore eschewed dependence on any particular style and pedantry. What was important for cottages was the living style of the local craftsmen. Where he felt most recent model cottages had failed was that they had been designed, but that local workmen had not been able to bring that design alive. They had remained the stereotypes of the pattern books. James was thus making a plea for craftsmanship which pre-dated the Arts and Crafts Movement of the later century with its profound impact on cottage style and design. Style, he urged, must arise from the simple elements of good cottage building:

> . . . we shall never have a real, living style, until we have imbued the workman with true principles in the use of the wood and the brick with which he makes the doors and cornices of his own dwelling . . . If we could once get true principles of carpentering into our cottages and our builders' workshops, we should have the base of a national style to work upon, and need have no fear of missing a right development. Now, in the commonest buildings, there is a waste of labour in bad forms and surface polish, which are much more costly than well proportioned realities . . . I believe that if we could, as a rule, get rid of all shams and false ornament in our cottages, improvement would gradually rise upwards, and our builders would not be, as now, working in a conventional groove of their own, unpermeated by any living principle, and with no sympathy with the higher art of the architect. It is on this ground that I would ask the most exalted architect not to deem cottage building beneath his care. I think he would there learn *reality*.

Such practical pre-occupations characterized James's determination of the actual accommodation required by the labourer:

> He wants a living room, a kitchen, and a pantry on the ground floor, and three bedrooms above, with out-house for wood, coals, offices, etc.; or, to describe the ground plan, as it is mostly and bestly used – a kitchen, which is also the living room and the largest room in the house, and a wash-house which serves as a back-kitchen in the summer, and which, if we were speaking of a large house, we should call the scullery. There is the pantry besides, and, if possible, a closet under the stairs. This is the ground plan required.

The point behind this planning was the realistic view that the labourer could only afford one fire at a time and that this should form both the kitchen range and the heating of the living-room. Having established one large room on the ground floor, it was necessary to make any other room, such as scullery, wash-house or pantry, so small that they could not be allowed any other than a service function:

My object, then, is not to allow of a company room in my model labourer's home; for it necessarily entails a sloppy, untidy, comfortless, everyday existence in the wash-house or scullery; but if you make this latter room so small that it cannot accommodate the family at their meals, if you put the kitchen range in the best room, have only a small hearth in the scullery with boiler and sink, then you make this back room what it should be, a place for washing, slopping, and 'doing', as they say, 'their jobs in', and you force the family to live ordinarily in the largest and wholesomest room, which necessitates certain more comely observances of civilised life, and helps to elevate the whole household in their social relations. The really tidy, good housewife, the good mother who takes pride in the cleanliness of her pets as well as of her pots, and likes to see her family in substantial comfort around her, will prefer this arrangement, though it implies a little more method, and entails a little more labour, to keep all things in their places in a room constantly occupied.

The problem posed by these practical requirements was that if there were to be three bedrooms on the first floor, then they had to be fitted into a ground area adequate simply for a living room, scullery and pantry. In trying to accommodate one storey to the other, either the bedrooms had to be cramped to a most inconvenient and unhealthy size, or the scullery had to be enlarged so as to make it into the general living-room, at a waste of space and money. To meet these concerns James set down the accommodation required for the married agricultural labour as follows:

. . . on the ground floor: 1. Dining room or kitchen in one; with a range containing oven and boiler, pot hooks, cupboard, light convenient for cooking, that is, on the side not facing the fireplace. Superficial area of not less than 168 ft. 2. Scullery with sink, copper, small hearth, fireplace, with outer door communicating with back yard, and another door communicating with passage, or, better with living room. Superficial area 96 ft. 3. Pantry with shelves and room for beer cask, window opening into the outer air, and in communication with passage or scullery. The three bedrooms, respectively, two about 108 ft. and one 90 ft. In round numbers, an area of about 300 ft. on each floor. The height of the lower rooms 8 ft., of the bedrooms the same, or 5 or 6 ft. on the walls, with the roof taken in. The best arrangement of this number of rooms is that which allows of an outer porch with inner lobby or passage, giving independent access to stairs, kitchen, pantry, and scullery, with landing upstairs admitting separate entrance to each of the three bedrooms.

The concern here was to return, in an architectural sense, to simplicity. The problem was that it took until the end of the century for such practical concerns, both with regard to the needs of the tenants and to the appearance of the buildings, to have an impact on both the design and style of model dwellings for labourers.

SOURCES

James, T. (1862) Labourers' cottages, and their bearing upon architecture. *Building News*, **IX**.
Strickland, C.W. (1864) *On Cottage Construction and Design*. Cambridge.

Bannister Fletcher's Model Houses, 1871

The architect, Bannister Fletcher, published his book, *Model Houses for the Industrial Classes*, in 1871, providing a review of the defects of existing houses and presenting 'model' designs, some of which had been erected as examples. He criticized the many attempts at model building which had taken place over the previous thirty years, particularly on the grounds that none of them provided an investment on ordinary paying principles. He concluded that 'the much-praised models are not initiated by independent persons, and that the general sentiment of the working people remains as ever, hopelessly against them'. Though he recognized the sanitary improvements which had been incorporated in these earlier models, he felt that the main problem was their generally expensive construction. Further he argued that they failed to take account of the feelings, wishes and health of the inhabitants; that the numbers housed in the large tenement blocks of model dwellings were too large to allow any privacy, and at the same time required supervision. In short, there had been a lack of understanding of the needs of working people or sympathy with their interests, habits and pre-occupations.

Following this indictment of the building profession, Bannister Fletcher tackled the subject in a practical way, analysing the defects of existing plans for model dwellings, with their extremely narrow staircases, the great loss of space in passages, the awkward shape of the rooms and the darkness of the living-rooms. The communal staircase was criticized because it forced strangers and neighbours together in the approach to people's homes and so destroyed the sense of privacy, which was considered essential to family life. These problems occurred in model dwellings largely because architects, and certainly good architects, did not consider working class housing as worthy of their attention.

In responding to this situation, Bannister Fletcher proposed a scheme which incorporated flats within a terrace whose external appearance resembled a set of ordinary lower middle class dwellings. In doing this he developed what was the only practical alternative in flat design to the high impersonal blocks of grim brickwork which characterized the tenements of the model dwellings companies; that was the concept of the two storey cottage flat. It was an approach that was traditionally common in Tyneside and had been adopted for model dwellings by the Edinburgh Co-operative Building Co. Ltd. in 1861, because it was particularly concerned to avoid the dark internal staircases of the usual Scottish tenement blocks.

In this system each house was two storey with a flat on each floor with its own

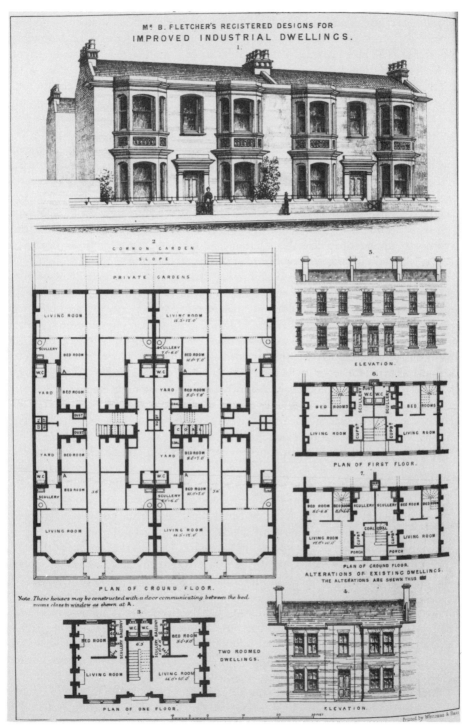

Mr B. FLETCHER'S REGISTERED DESIGNS FOR
IMPROVED INDUSTRIAL DWELLINGS.

separate entrance. Bannister Fletcher adapted this approach to conform with the
current conventions of London housing, and in order to ensure an acceptable
appearance. The plan provided a simple solution in grouping together two terraces
with yards and service areas in between, and then connecting them together with
internal corridors which gave access to four self-contained dwellings on the ground
floor, and then by a staircase set half-way down its length to four more dwellings on
the second floor. Such a plan thereby limited the number of families using the
common access corridor and at the same time allowed for the careful disposal of well-
shaped, spacious, airy and light rooms, with the suitable location of water closets,
coal houses and dust containers adjoining an internal yard or balcony, which formed a
miniature back-yard in the case of the upstairs flats. This arrangement overcame two
of the problems associated with the large blocks of model dwellings in which such
facilities were shared and continuous balconies obscured the light from adjoining
rooms. In addition, it ensured the minimum requirements of sanitarians that the
lavatory should not open directly off a room and should be separated from the rest of
the dwelling and be properly ventilated. The central corridor secured through ventilation which had been lacking with internal staircases.

This layout was designed to ensure maximum privacy within the constraints of
economy in both land and building. At the same time, it was incorporated within a
structure whose external appearance closely resembled a normal terrace, with
nothing to show that the building was occupied by more than one family. As against
the ordinary terrace, however, the considerable depth of the property in relation to
its width allowed for economy in the land occupied; compared with the large blocks
of model dwellings capital costs were much lower. The example erected at Penton-
ville cost £1118 for a unit of eight dwellings. These were let at 7s. 6d. per week for
the back sets and 8s. 6d. for the front sets, thus giving a gross rental of £166 8s. per
annum which Fletcher argued presented a return on capital of 8½ per cent. This
compared very favourably with contemporary rentals in the district for terraced
houses, which averaged at 4s. 9d. a room. It was also contrasted with the consequences of other model dwellings where 'five per cent philanthropy' resulted in rents
for a single room of around 2s. 1¼d. per week and of 5s. 6d. for two rooms.

The benefits of this model were, however, achieved by means of a design that
revolved around an internal courtyard which, despite the careful planning, brought
its own problems of circulation of air, dirt and noise. Though the concept of the two
storey cottage flat was widely taken up in the North and provided the basis for several
model schemes in the provinces, this metropolitan adaptation found little favour. It
was, nevertheless, a genuine attempt to respond to the sensibilities of the working-
class and to achieve an acceptable compromise between the large tenement block and
the self-contained cottage. As such it aroused considerable interest amongst architects and in 1875 *The Architect*, continuing its attack on barrack block dwellings,
promoted the idea. It also brought to the fore the need for flexibility of design within
the scope of any model.

Thus Fletcher presented plans for different sizes of flats, and in the three
bedroomed flat provided separate access to one of the bedrooms so it could be let off if

necessitated by family and financial circumstances. He also advocated the adaptation of existing terraces in order to incorporate improved dwellings for the working classes. This was a move towards the recognition of the reality of housing and the need for model schemes to take account of the circumstances of the poor and their continued occupation of older properties built for other purposes.

SOURCES

The Architect, **XIV**, 1875.

Building News, **XXI**, 1871.

Fletcher, B.F. (1871) *Model Houses for the Industrial Classes*. London: Longman.

Case Study Seven

Bye-Law Housing

The influence of the debates of housing reformers with regard to the laying down of minimum standards of construction, as well as of space and light was tentatively expressed in many provincial bye-law codes during the course of the 1860s. The ideas were embodied at a national level in the Public Health Act of 1875. Under Section 157 of that Act local authorities were empowered, though still not compelled, to make bye-laws with regard to the control of new streets, their width and construction, and the erection of new buildings, the regulation of the space around them and their sanitary requirements.

In order to set a standard at which these clauses might be interpreted, the Local Government Board produced a series of model bye-laws as a guide to local authorities who wished to adopt the Act and use its powers to enforce acceptable standards of housing development. The local authority could not, however, be forced to make bye-laws but when it did its code of bye-laws had to be ratified by the Local Government Board, who were therefore able to impose a certain uniformity of standards. These had been worked out in consultation with the Royal Institute of British Architects and were circularized by the Local Government Board in 1877 as its 'New Code of Model Bye-Laws'.

This code included clauses dealing with light and ventilation within the dwellings themselves by governing the size of windows in relation to the amount of internal floor space and the number of opening windows, though they did not attempt to regulate room heights.

The bye-laws provided controls over the construction of houses, affecting foundations, building materials, thickness of walls, strength of floors and safety of chimneys. There were also clauses affecting sanitary objects. Drains were to be properly ventilated, embedded in concrete and laid in direct lines under houses. Closets were to be placed so that at least one side was an external wall and were provided with constant ventilation. Alternative sanitary arrangements were catered for in great detail.

However, those sections of the model bye-laws that had most effect on the appearance and overall quality of housing, and thereby established a minimum model, were the regulations governing streets, open spaces around buildings and the height of buildings. In order to secure the proper ventilation of buildings by the free circulation of air around them the model bye-laws were primarily concerned with the minimum amount of space left open adjoining a house:

> Every person who shall erect a new domestic building shall provide on the front of such building an open space which shall be free from any erection thereon above the level of

Terraced housing built under Manchester's model bye-laws.

the ground, except any portico, porch, steps or other like projection from such building or any gate, fence or wall not exceeding seven feet in height, and which measured to the boundary of any lands or premises immediately opposite, or to the opposite side of any street which such buildings may face shall, throughout the whole line of the frontage of such buildings, extend to a distance of 24 feet at the least, such distance being measured in every case at right angles to the external face of any wall of such buildings which should front or abut on such open space. A person who shall make any alteration or addition to such building shall not, by such alteration or addition, diminish the extent of open space provided in pursuance of this bye-law in connection with such building.

By this clause development was to be regulated so that all houses had to have an open space in front equal to the minimun width of the street, and they could no longer be built haphazardly in courts and alleys. This spatial control was further strengthened by the imposition of restrictions on building to the rear of the house:

Every person who shall erect a new domestic building shall provide in the rear of such building an open space exclusively belonging to such building and of an aggregate extent of not less than 150 square feet and free from any erection thereon above the level of the ground, except a water-closet, earth-closet or privy and an ash pit. He shall cause such open space to extend laterally throughout the entire width of such building and he shall cause the distance across such open space from every point of such building to the boundary of any lands and premises immediately opposite and adjoining the site of such building to be not less in any case than 10 feet. If the height of such building be 15 feet he shall cause such distance to be 15 feet at least. If the height of such building be 25 feet he shall cause such distance to be 25 feet at least. If the height of such building be 35 feet or exceed 35 feet he shall cause such distance to be 35 feet at the least.

This clause, by stating that the open land attached to a house should be definitely to the rear of the building and not alternatively at the side, sought to secure the absolute prevention of back-to-back building. A loophole in many earlier bye-laws had allowed the required open space to adjoin the house simply on one side while the other was built up.

The circulation of air within a housing development was to be secured by wide open streets with frequent intersections. The model bye-laws required that all new streets should be of a minimum width of 36 feet, except for those which were less than 100 feet long, and these could be treated as pedestrian roads with a reduced width of 24 feet. All streets were to be open at one end throughout their full width and height, and not to exceed 100 yards in length without an opening of equal width across the whole street. The model bye-laws did not, however, include any provision for the control of back streets, though the nature of the requirements for open space at the rear of buildings meant that the back street became a common feature of housing built under these bye-laws.

The standards of layout suggested by the model bye-laws were not, however, rapidly adopted. On the one hand, the provisions of the Public Health Act did not apply to London, while on the other, many provincial towns operated bye-laws which had been formulated under the powers of a local act and were not, therefore, subject to the supervision of the Local Government Board. Such local powers allowed authorities to be much more lenient than the Board advocated. In the West Riding towns of Leeds, Bradford and Halifax, for instance, the retention of powers granted under earlier local acts enabled the authorities to continue to allow the building of back-to-back houses, though admittedly under regulations as to the continuity and density of development. Some towns rapidly adopted new bye-laws under the Public Health Act which reached the appropriate standards of the Local Government Board. Most towns, however, gradually brought their local bye-laws into conformity with the model code and tightened the wording of existing building regulations in order to bring practice into line with theory. In most cases, therefore, the result was that by the time of the Royal Commission on the Housing of the Working Classes (1884–5), apart from certain local anomalies, housing and urban expansion was proceeding in provincial centres basically in accordance with the standards prescribed under the 1875 Public Health Act.

This resulted in the last decades of the nineteenth century in bye-law housing which spread over large areas of working class suburbs and which commonly consisted of repetitive terraces of houses, each with a small walled yard containing a privy and perhaps a coal house. These were set in long parallel treeless streets. The front doors of the houses opened directly onto the street, except in those better class ones where there might be a small front garden. Such housing has been much criticized on account of its monotony and the dreary and depressing uniformity of the environment it created. The bye-laws did not, however, require monotonous layout and dreary design, and regulations in themselves cannot be blamed if society chooses to house its population as cheaply as possible and thereby in identical terraces of housing. What is important is that the model bye-laws provided a model

The impact of bye-law regulations on spatial standards and housing layout.

of minimum standards, and thereby ensured that houses built under the bye-laws were at least healthy and adequately built, and were laid out with more space, greater openness and better circulation. To this extent housing built under the model bye-laws represented a distinct advance in working class housing standards.

SOURCES

Chambers, G.F. (1887) *A Digest of the Law Relating to Public Health and Local Government. Annotated Model Bye-Laws.* London: C. Knight, 1883.

Lumley, W.G. & E. (1876) *The Public Health Act 1875.* London: Shaw.

The Model Village: Bournville

W.A. Harvey, the architect of the original development at Bournville, described its development in *The Model Village and its Cottages: Bournville* (1906), and discussed its underlying rationale:

> The housing problem is no longer one in which the poor in the congested districts of great towns are alone concerned. A far larger section is affected – a section which includes not only the labouring class, but also the skilled artisan and even a class of the people still more prosperous. In the light of present sanitary and hygienic knowledge it is at last recognised that the housing conditions of the past will not suffice for the future . . . Whether land is developed privately or by public bodies, it is essential, in order to secure real reform, that the needs, domestic and social, of the people for whom the houses are provided should be entirely understood. What will have to be provided are *homes* . . .

The inference of this was that the accommodation provided in the house was not the only matter of concern, but that close attention should also be given to the environment, which must be healthy and pleasant. The stimulation for this rejuvenation in the physical appearance and environmental control of housing during the last decades of the century came from the ideas of Morris and Lethaby, which were transmitted in architectural terms by Philip Webb and his followers. In practice, the first examples of the application of new ideas to working class housing came from the industrial settlement of Bournville begun in 1879 and later from Port Sunlight begun in 1888. The original Bournville village occupied 118 acres and adjoined the area covered by Cadbury Bros' factory, which with its recreation grounds occupied another 165 acres. The average plot allowed for each house was about 500 yd², and there was a space of 82 ft from house front to house front. The roads were tree-lined and 16 acres were devoted to open spaces. Here was established the town-country scale that was to govern the layout of later garden suburbs. In Bournville, and later at Port Sunlight, great attention was paid to the special qualities of layout – the straight street of the bye-law terrace was discarded in favour of a picturesque settlement of trees and gardens, with cottages built semi-detached or disposed of in units of five or six. The roads themselves lost the ridigity of the grid iron, for as Harvey commented: ' . . . it is nearly always better to work to the contour of the land, taking a general sweep in preference to a straight line'.

These pre-conditions anticipated two of the later principles of Parker and Unwin

Cottages at Bournville as they appeared in the original layout.

that were to guide the development of the garden suburb – low density on the land (5 to 8 houses per acre at Port Sunlight and 7 to 8 at Bournville), and a reduction in the number of streets necessary for residential developments. The model houses of the two villages also provided object lessons in grouping and design. A greater diversity of textures and colours was evidence of a desire for variety in the street picture. At Bournville the different Staffordshire bricks, the handmade tiles and careful roof ridging were all incorporated in order to obtain 'that rustic appearance suitable to a cottage', and were in definite reaction to the turgid repetition of the Birmingham bye-law streets. At Port Sunlight, the variety of materials and styles was even more impressive, though the danger of disintegration was avoided by the construction of up to ten house-units within mansion blocks which were designed so that there was the minimum of external demarcation between individual houses. These larger units provided new opportunities for grouping around open spaces and developing the street scene. Planning devices were forecast which were to be incorporated in the Garden City concept.

Though Bournville and Port Sunlight both foreshadowed the type of layout that was to influence future suburban planning, neither resulted in immediate imitation. Primarily this was a result of problems of economic viability. Lever never made any secret of the fact that the rents received at Port Sunlight did not cover the charges incurred. In that sense the development was, under the terms used in this book, an ideal rather than a model development. At Bournville, Cadbury always intended that the rents received should show a 5 per cent return on capital and that the village should stand as a practical example and model for others. The problem, however, was that which had bedevilled Victorian housing reform all along, of providing houses at rents within the means of the poorer working man.

W.A. Harvey tackled this problem with careful consideration for economy in design and cost of materials, as well as for the pleasing effect aimed at:

> With regard to the house itself, so far as it contributes to a pleasant environment, it should be remembered that architectural beauty is not dependent upon the ornament introduced; on the contrary, the use of the latter rather tends to deprive the dwelling of its homeliness, and of this truth, the jerry-built house, with its scroll-cut lintel and moulded brick string course, affords only too frequent an illustration. The soul of beauty is harmony which may co-exist with the veriest simplicity; and it is in the harmonious treatment of parts, not in useless and sometimes costly decoration, that a dwelling gains that homely appearance which it should be our aim to realise.

Elevation of cottages in blocks of eight.

In pursuit of this model, Harvey put forward plans for cottages in blocks of eight costing £135 each. These were not erected at Bournville because of the decision of the Village Trust not to build in blocks of more than four, for which the cost was stated as £160 per cottage. The elevation of these designs for blocks of eight illustrates the way in which economy of construction was sought without sacrificing that privacy and homeliness considered essential to the cottage home. Nevertheless, the cost was more than that of the contemporary speculative working class house. Harvey, however, pointed out that it was not fair to compare simply building costs, but maintenance costs also had to be taken into account. He stressed, therefore, the need for proper foundations and ventilated damp courses, as well as the use wherever possible of stock articles and the standardization of timbers and other fittings. Added to these economies of construction was the concern for simplicity and regularity and planning. Thus the roof runs uninterruptedly from end to end, by which unnecessary roof complications are avoided; the eaves run uninterruptedly for the windows are not allowed to complicate the guttering and tiling by breaking through the roof line. The height of the building was also reduced to the lowest limit; 8 ft 3 in for the ground floor and 8 ft for the bedroom floor were considered sufficient providing there was adequate ventilation.

Thus at the same time, the scale of the building was made more pleasing and there was legitimate economy in the brickwork. In the example given, the staircase runs between the houses and gives them a good wide frontage and allows all the cottages access to a reasonable sized yard and garden. The interior fittings were of the simplest

Cottage bath in the kitchen floor.

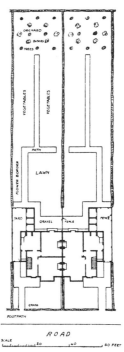

Model layout for gardens at Bournville.

and most inexpensive kind; such things as an inglenook, however desirable, being reserved for better class cottages. The bath in these smaller cottages was of the 'cabinet' patent type which was easily shut up and stowed away. Nevertheless, ample cupboard room was provided and conveniences such as cloak and picture rails, hooks and shelves were fixed in all the cottages, along with a small gas cooker. The essentials of these model houses were adequate accommodation, including minimum bathroom and kitchen standards, combined with a pleasing and harmonious exterior appearance.

In addition to the design and building of the house itself, great care and attention was given to the planning of the garden which was considered of such importance in a model village. The accompanying plan was one frequently adopted at Bournville, though the arrangement was modified in the case of the smaller cottages by the reduction or omission of turf. Trees and shrubs were provided, as well as hedges and creepers, with a view to providing a screen between the houses as well as enhancing the general effect. It was in this context that Harvey summed up the significance of Bournville as a model:

> If it be asked, with regard to the problem of the housing of the people what is Bournville's contribution towards its solution, it would be stating its claims at the lowest to say that it stands as an example of what the village of the future may be, a village of healthy homes amid pleasant surroundings where fresh air is abundant and beauty present, and where are secured to its people by an administration co-operative in nature numerous benefits which under present circumstances are denied them elsewhere.

SOURCES

Bournville Village Trust (1956) *1900–1955*. Bournville: Bournville Village Trust.

Harvey, W.A. (1906) *The Model Village and its Cottages: Bournville*. London: Batsford.

Whitehouse, J.H. (1902) Bournville: a study in housing reform. *Studio*, **XXIV**.

Case Study Nine

Block Dwellings, 1895

The last decade of the nineteenth century was, as Tarn has observed, a period of growing optimism that the housing problem would be solved. There was a wave of fresh activity, in part due to the greater involvement of local authorities after the Housing of the Working Classes Act of 1890:

> . . . the country was ready to move into the new century as a more responsible society: the battles for the control of building development, spatially and sanitarily, and for state interference in an effort to solve the housing problem were won, at least in theory, and it was only the method of effectively implementing the new policies which remained to be fully worked out after 1890.

In that process there appeared over the following decade a spate of monographs from housing reformers, architects and sanitarians. Recognizing the need to maintain the impetus and to bring models of best practice to the attention of public opinion, Edward Bowmaker, a medical practitioner, published his *Housing of the Working Classes* in 1895. This brought together material scattered through various journals and reports, and demonstrated what could be achieved and what should be aimed at by both public bodies and private individuals.

Bowmaker accepted as axiomatic that the only means of re-housing on slum clearance sites was by means of some form of block dwellings. He recognized the traditional objections to these in terms of their ugliness, their imposition of collective arrangements, their rapid deterioration, and their occupation by people for whom they were not intended. He accepted that some existing block dwellings were unsatisfactory and that the need was to design dwellings which were also homes.

It was accepted that almost everyone desired a self-contained dwelling for his family. Nevertheless, economy necessitated some dwellings in which the conveniences were shared by the occupants of several homes. Separate tenements, whilst the most satisfactory system, could only be secured in those blocks in which the higher rentals could be obtained. If, however, it was absolutely necessary to adopt this type of block for the use of those who could afford only the smallest outlay for rent, then the disadvantages could be reduced to a minimum by limiting the use of the convenience to as small groups of tenants as possible.

Whatever type of block was erected, it was argued that, in addition to the ordinary sanitary conveniences, it was important that laundry and bath accommodation should be provided and that this might, with considerable advantage, be arranged to supply the whole of a block, accessible at certain fixed times to each of the tenants. In many cases reading and recreation rooms had also been supplied, but it was felt that these might fairly be classed as luxuries, which must materially tend to an increased cost.

At the same time, special provisions were required in the case of block dwellings in order that they might not be erected on principles prejudicial to health:

> Requirements which are perfectly satisfactory in the case of smaller houses, are naturally inadequate to meet the demands of huge blocks . . . To continue to erect large blocks of dwellings without taking adequate precautions to obtain space around the buildings, sufficiently wide and open to prevent their overshadowing each other, and to provide for the through lighting of the houses, particularly the lower ones, by the direct rays of the sun, is to seriously endanger the public health. Light and air are necessary to the health of the people and the inadequate provision of these necessities has a most disastrous effect upon their constitutions.

Various estimates had been made as to the amount of open space required around block dwellings. The London Building Act of 1894 now prescribed that no such building should be erected 'within the prescribed distance to a height exceeding the distance of the front or nearest external wall on the opposite side of the street'. Fixing the distance between two buildings at the height of the highest, these provisions were far in advance of previous requirements and demonstrated official recognition of the problem of space around blocks.

The same Act limited the height of any new building in London to 80 ft. Bowmaker advised that this was far too high for block buildings, a desirable maximum being 60 ft, which allowed six storeys. Smaller blocks might with advantage be constructed, and he noted with satisfaction the decision of the London County Council to limit their blocks to five storeys. With regard to the layout of dwellings:

> The buildings should be erected in straight rows, with only slight projections or indentations, in order to allow free play of air and sunlight on every part of the dwelling. This arrangement is preferable to the square. Where such projections contain the sanitary accommodation, it is important that cross-lighting and cross-ventilation should be secured. It is essential that through ventilation or perflation should be as perfect as possible, and that all passages or staircases should be well lighted. The latter demands most careful attention; one of the most serious objections to existing blocks is that in a very large number of cases the passages and staircases are dark and badly ventilated. This in many recent buildings is obviated by making the staircases open to the air, and protected by an iron railing. The lining of passages and staircases with white glazed bricks renders them light even on a dull day. Corridors are undesirable, and wherever possible should be avoided.

Turning to the amount of accommodation to be provided, Bowmaker recognized that this would vary according to needs, but estimated that tenements of two or three rooms would be most eagerly sought after. Above this number the rentals would necessarily prevent working men from occupying them. A certain proportion of single-room tenements would be required, though it was felt that their construction should not be encouraged more than was absolutely necessary. Every single

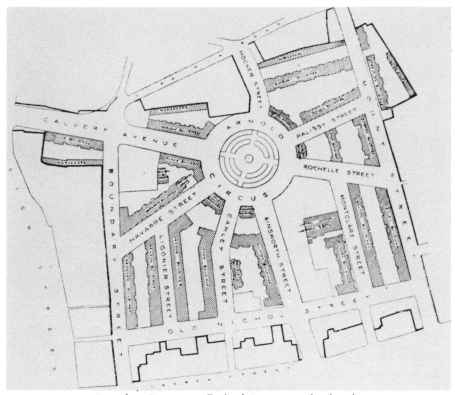

Boundary Street area, Bethnal Green, as redeveloped.

room should have a minimum superficial area of 140 ft^2 and each additional room should have at least 96 ft^2. The London Building Act 1894 provided that all habitable rooms should be at least 8 ft 6 in high, but Bowmaker advised that in moderate size rooms 10 ft was desirable in order to facilitate ventilation. It was important that rooms in upper storeys should not be of less height than those of the lower. All staircases and landings should not be less than 3 ft 6 in wide. The amount of window space should be calculated on the basis of 20 ft^2 of window area to every 1200 ft^3 of room space. Finally, Bowmaker urged care and attention in the erection of these dwellings. Unless erected substantially, blocks of dwellings deteriorated very rapidly, despite careful management. If model dwellings were to be models, local authorities needed to supervize and control their erection.

As examples of the two types of block dwellings identified, Bowmaker provided descriptions of the LCC scheme then in the course of erection at Boundary Street in Bethnal Green.

Self-contained dwellings have been provided comprising one, two, three, and four rooms. By far the larger proportion consists of two or three rooms; it being considered that these will be more eagerly sought after. The front door of each dwelling opens on the

Boundary Street flats from the central circus.

CLEEVE BUILDINGS, BOUNDARY STREET ESTATE.
PLAN No. 28.

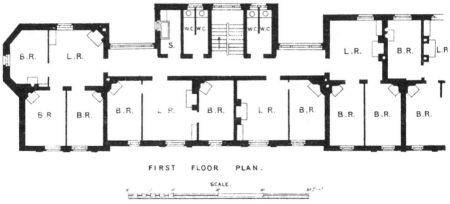

FIRST   FLOOR   PLAN.

SCALE.

Plan showing disposition of rooms in typical self-contained block dwelling.

ground floor directly from a wide passage, and in the upper storeys from the landing of the staircase. The living room is 13 ft. 7 in. by 11 ft. 4 in. and is fitted with a Cundy grate, in which the oven is below the fire. Across the corner of the room against the outer wall is a ventilated food cupboard, and a dresser is provided with a coal box, shelves, and drawers. Half a dozen coat pegs are fixed to a rail on the wall. This room is so arranged that a bed can be conveniently placed, it being necessary to use it as a bedroom when the family is large. The living room communicates with the bedrooms, one to the front and one towards the back of the house; but in the case of two-roomed tenements, the front bedroom is dispensed with. The back bedroom is 12 ft. 3 in. by 8 ft. 6 in.; the front being 12 ft. 10 in. by 7 ft. 10 in. No fittings are provided in the bedrooms. At the back, the living room opens into a scullery provided with a sink, a copper and a towel roller; and through an open lobby access is got to the water closet, which is thus entirely cut off from the house. With the latter great care has been taken, and the drainage has been most thoroughly carried out. The closets are of the 'wash-down' type, set in concrete, and flushed with two gallons of water. The soil pipes are set outside the building, and they are thoroughly ventilated, as are also the waste pipes from the sculleries. Dust shoots are provided so that the dust and dry refuse can be efficiently removed from the dwellings.

These houses, which very aptly illustrate the self-contained principle, are intended for persons earning about 21/- per week, and have cost the council on an average £80 a room, a sum very considerably beyond the average usually allowed for such dwellings. The work is being most thoroughly carried out, and there can be no doubt that very shortly one of the most wretched slums will have given place to dwellings of a most satisfactory nature.

Associated dwellings. Blocks of the second type are also to be erected, in which on the score of cheapness the sculleries and w.c.s are used in common. The amount of accommodation provided resembles the dwellings we have just described.

The dwellings are entered from a corridor; and to each floor sculleries are provided with a sufficient number of sinks, also water closets for the use of women and children. Dust shoots are provided as before. It is probable that a central laundry will be erected for the use of the tenants. The dwellings are not to be compared with the self-contained tenements we have described, but where cheapness is important, in order to make provision for the *very poor*, nothing better could be desired.

In its variety of accommodation and standards of construction, the Boundary Street scheme stood as a model of the principles and practices which Bowmaker was advocating. The advance achieved in that model has been estimated by Tarn:

The internal planning of the dwellings followed the precedents already established by other organisations, except that there was a definite attempt to increase the standard of accommodation within the individual tenement both in terms of the size of rooms and their number . . . The scheme was important, however, for other reasons than merely halting a downward tendency which was noticeable in much contemporary work. It was a very large development, and consequently it was possible to exercise proper spatial control, to pursue a planning policy . . . It was no longer a matter of simply juggling with a standard block on an unencumbered piece of land, the buildings were designed especially for the site, and they related architecturally to each other as well as to the larger conception of the estate. Furthermore, there was provision for open space, both in the central raised garden and also between certain of the blocks, so that the usual pattern of building separated by paved wastes was abolished . . . The third quality which the scheme possessed was that of a new architectural sensitivity, new, that is, to the housing movement. At last the barrack-like block which had characterised working class housing for half a century was replaced by a more humane type of design . . . Boundary Street was a new experience in housing architecture.

SOURCES

Bowmaker, E. (1895) *Housing of the Working Classes*. London: Methuen.

London County Council (1901) *The Housing Question in London*. London: London County Council.

Tarn, J.N. (1973) *Five Per Cent Philanthropy: An Account of Housing in Urban Areas between 1840 and 1914*. London: Cambridge University Press.

Cottage Plans and Common Sense, 1902

Raymond Unwin calculated that the desirable number of cottages, from the point of view of health and comfort, would be between ten and twelve houses per acre. Near the centre of a town, this number would necessarily be higher, but he felt that it need not exceed twenty, and that wherever possible the number should be restricted to between ten and twelve.

> Twelve houses to the net acre of building land, excluding all roads, has been proved to be about the right number to give gardens of sufficient size to be of commercial value to the tenants – large enough, that is, to be worth cultivating seriously for the sake of profit, and not too large to be worked by an ordinary labourer and his family.

In his pamphlet *Nothing Gained by Overcrowding*, Unwin contrasted a plot of ten acres with 34 houses per acre with another of 15.2 houses per acre. In the first scheme each house had 83½ yd² of ground, while in the second scheme the lower density allowed each house 261½ yd². The roads in the first scheme would have cost £9,747.10/- compared with £4,480 in the second scheme. The result was that, though the number of houses had been reduced by half, the plot sizes had been tripled and the layout cost per house remained stable. As Creese has pointed out, it was not actually a principle of costing less that counted, so much as obtaining more for the money per family unit.

In addition to economies in layout, this freer development also made possible the rethinking of the plan of the house or working class cottage. The houses described by Raymond Unwin in *Cottage Plans and Common Sense*, and subsequently developed by him on the earliest part of the estate at New Earswick (begun 1902), adapted to working class homes many of the innovations of Webb and of Voysey. In place of the narrow fronted terraced house with a front and back room, the lower streetage costs enabled the evolution of houses with greater widths. This meant that, in the first place, it was possible to provide more variety in accommodation. Secondly, all the accommodation required was brought under the main roof, and long back projections or detached out-buildings were dispensed with, which effected a reduction of gloom and shade. Thirdly, the increased wall space admitted more windows and allowed staircases, landings and larders to be placed on outer walls with direct light and ventilation. Lastly, the proportions of the buildings lent themselves to a treatment more pleasing to the eye. Breadth itself is a valuable aesthetic quality and when it was associated with the broad casement window of simple framing and the long

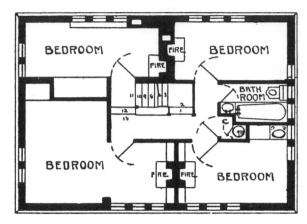

FIRST FLOOR PLAN

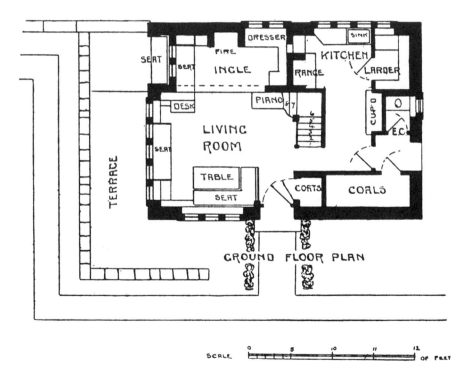

GROUND FLOOR PLAN

SCALE

Cottage designed for a site in Derbyshire by Barry Parker and Raymond Unwin.

lines of a well-pitched roof, then to some degree there was recovered the homely
appearance of the English country cottage.

These features were, however, not just a consequence of aesthetic considerations, but also resulted from the practical approach advocated to the designing of small houses and cottages. In this Unwin considered the site the most important factor as it suggested both the internal arrangement and external treatment. The house should be sited so as to provide the occupants with a pleasing view, while at the same time ensuring that it harmonized with its surroundings. To this end Unwin advocated that the surroundings should determine both the colour and the form of the house. As greatly as the site influenced the external treatment of the house, it even more definitely affected its internal arrangements. It was argued that the most important thing was to so plan as to bring plenty of sunshine into all the main rooms of the house:

> . . . the importance of arranging for the few days when the sun is oppressive is small indeed compared with that of planning to suit the many days when every hour of sunshine is of utmost value. The general rule, then, would seem to be, so to contrive as to get the sunshine into a room at a time when it is most likely to be occupied.

This led to the providing of living-rooms with a south or south-west aspect, a kitchen to the east or north-east, bathrooms and bedrooms similarly with an eastern aspect where possible. It was recognized however that such considerations of aspect would internally have to be modified in individual circumstances in order to ensure the best prospect and most pleasant outlook.

A further advantage which arose from giving aspect its due weight was the consequent abolition of back-yards and back-alleys. Criticizing them as areas out of sight where rubbish was collected, and as dreary, sunless playgrounds for children, Unwin castigated the squalid ugliness of the back-yard and the lack of prospect that it offered. In its place every house must have some space to itself:

> If, instead of being wasted in separate yards and dirty back streets, space which is available for a number of houses were kept together, it would make quite a respectable square or garden. The cottages could then be grouped round such open spaces, forming quadrangles opening one into the other, with wide streets at intervals . . . At present it is too often the custom to draw out a cottage plan that will come within a certain space and then repeat unaltered street after street, heedless of whether it faces north, south, east or west. Nothing more absurd or more regardless of essential conditions could be imagined.

The consideration of such concerns was to lead Unwin to the advocacy of the quadrangle as a model form of layout which would lift the group of cottages out of the common place and give them some dignity. The distance across would ensure the essential privacy for each home, while the central area would provide a safe place for children to play, and at the same time effect 'a pleasant and interesting outlook for all the cottages'.

Having so sited and arranged the houses as to be in the best interests of the self-contained dwelling, Unwin directed attention to the organization and utilization of the house. He recognized that within the tight financial constraints governing the

Illus. 292.—Hampstead Garden Suburb. Sketch showing quadrangle of medium-sized houses. For plan see Illus. 277.

Raymond Unwin's ideas for the layout of model cottages put into practice at Hampstead Garden Suburb.

construction of cottages, it was not possible to give each house what might in abstract be desirable. This did not mean, however, that the ideal of cottage accommodation should not be considered. It was a matter of adapting this to the model which could be afforded:

> Except by a very careful study of the life which that space is to shelter, it is not possible to design the house so as to properly fit and accommodate that life, and it is only by making the house fit the life of its occupants that a right and economical use of the space can be obtained.

Unwin then noted some of the requirements for different rooms in the house:

> *Living-room.* The first consideration in planning any cottage should be to provide a roomy, convenient and comfortable living-room, having a sunny aspect and a cheerful outlook . . . It is very important to plan a living-room so that the doors or staircases may not destroy the comfort, or even the sense of comfort. They should be kept away from the fire, and, above all, should not open across either the fire or the window . . . in planning the room the furniture should always be arranged and drawn in, to make sure that provision has been made for work and rest, for meals and play.

> *Bedrooms.* After the living-room, the sleeping rooms must be regarded as next in importance, for these will be occupied all night. Of these it is only needfull to say that they should be as large as can be provided, and as well ventilated as possible. There should be plenty of windows, easily opened, and everything possible done to encourage the opening of them. If the room can be arranged so that there should be a comfortable corner between fire and window, where a quiet hour with book or pen can be spent, this is very desirable. For there is no reason why the accommodation of the small house should not be increased by a more general use of the bedrooms for these purposes.

Parlour. However desirable a parlour may be, it cannot be said to be necessary for health or family life; nor can it be compared in importance with those rooms and offices which we have been considering. There can be no possible doubt that until any cottage has been provided with a living-room large enough to be healthy, comfortable and convenient, it is worse than folly to take space from that living-room, where it will be used every day and every hour to form a parlour where it will only be used once or twice a week . . . Anyone who has known what it is to occupy a large airy house-place will not easily sacrifice its advantages for either a needless parlour or a useless passage . . . A desire to imitate the middle class house is at the bottom of the modern tendency to cut the cottage up into a series of minute compartments.

Bathroom. A bathroom for every cottage is an ideal which some day will surely come to be regarded as essential. In small tenements where the cost of this ideal may still be prohibitive, there seems no reason why there should not be provided at least a bathroom to each quadrangle.

Beyond these basic concerns, and beyond the house itself, Unwin felt that much could be achieved in his model through co-operation and the use of communal facilities – wash-houses, sculleries, drying grounds, playrooms and playgrounds, baths and communal centres. For Unwin the ideal was the self-contained cottage in its own plot of land; but he realized that the common sense model was the achievement of the best of this ideal within the constraints of the suburb and limitations of finance:

In municipal housing schemes, which spring from the co-operative efforts of the whole town or city, it would seem fitting that something should be done to foster associated action amongst the tenants and this is the more urgent because it is only by such association that we can hope to provide for the many some of the most desirable conveniences of life which wealth now enables the few to secure for themselves individually.

SOURCES

Parker, R.B. & Unwin, R. (1901) *The Art of Building a Home*. London: Longman.

Unwin, R. (1902) *Cottage Plans and Common Sense*. London: Fabian Tract.

Unwin, R. (1912) *Nothing Gained by Overcrowding! How the Garden City Type of Development may benefit both Owner and Occupier*. London: King.

Garden City
Cheap Cottage Exhibition, 1905

In 1905 a competitive exhibition of cheap cottages was organized at Letchworth Garden City with the intention of bringing to light a satisfactory example costing £150. This amount was laid down as the maximum a landowner could afford to spend on building, given that he could not expect to get more than 3s. a week, that is £8 per year, in rent from a rural labourer.

The exhibition did not succeed in this prime objective. Though, technically, cottages were erected for the amounts specified, they could not be reproduced at that price commercially, taking into account architects' fees and builders' profits, and allowing for normal costs of land and materials. As Lawrence Weaver reflected, 'If, then, anyone supposes that the exhibition solved the question in fact, as it appeared to do on paper, he is labouring under a delusion'. Even the cottage awarded first prize and built by Percy Houfton, the architect of the Woodlands Garden Village, could not be reproduced for less than £250.

As the periodical, *Garden City*, reported, the exhibition pricked the bubble of the £150 cottage. Nevertheless it was an experiment that brought up some useful features in planning and design. These were reviewed by the *Garden City* in the aftermath of the exhibition, against a series of practical questions regarding model cottages.

1. Is it possible to erect an iron cottage as cheaply as a brick cottage in a brick producing area?

Without taking into consideration the relevant merits of iron and brick for cottage building purposes, it might be said that where bricks did not exceed 25/- per thousand, the advantage in point of cost would be on the side of bricks.

The method of building cottages with an iron frame, especially when of the bungalow type, has not received from the public that amount of attention which it deserves. Such a cottage, covered on the outside with expanded metal, cement, plaster, and rough cast, and on the inside with expanded metal and ordinary plaster, and built upon a solid concrete base, results in a building of quite exceptional strength, great weather-resisting power, secures a fairly equable inside temperature and involves only a minimal expenditure in upkeep. It need not lack artistic attraction, and is practically fire proof. Under any circumstances, the cost will be very little in excess of a brick cottage, and this method may be strongly recommended for consideration in rural districts where bricks are expensive, or where cottages are to be built in an exposed position.

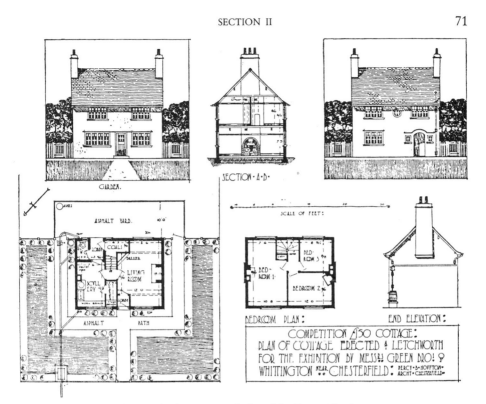

Prize-winning cottage designed by Percy Houfton.

2. What are the varying degrees of stability of patent materials, other than concrete blocks, and how do they compare with brick?

Probably no patent material has fully demonstrated its suitability for cottage building. The varieties of fibro-asbestos sheets or plates, of which Uralite is one of the best known, are all in some degree unsatisfactory. They are not in themselves readily adapted to taking various shapes or designs; a frame according to the required design has first to be erected, and these plates are merely fixed on. The main defect is that they are much too easily damaged, and not easily or cheaply repaired, and this is a vital matter in the case of cottages. Another defect is that while they afford fairly good protection from the heat, they are not equally effective against cold. It must be further admitted that in appearance they do not please the eye.

The 'Mack' is another interesting form of patent material; but this, too, has its failings. In the first place, the ordinary variety is not always successful in keeping out the wet, even with the addition of cement roughcast. No doubt by adding a tile facing this defect may practically be removed, but at the same time the cost will be considerably increased, and thus prevent the material from entering seriously into competition with bricks.

3. How do concrete hollow blocks compare with bricks as to price, and are they likely to be permanent and waterproof?

Artist's impression of a cottage by the Concrete Machinery Co. designed by G. Fraser.

Concrete hollow blocks form perhaps the most interesting feature of the recent cottage building experiment. It cannot yet be said that in point of costs they are equal, much less superior, to bricks; but it has been demonstrated that they are a useful alternative, even where bricks are moderately cheap. In districts where bricks are expensive, or where rough weather is frequently experienced, concrete blocks may then enter into serious, if not successful competition with brick . . . Is it durable, and will it keep out the weather? A categorical answer to either of these questions is impossible. Concrete, when used for building purposes, must be in competent hands . . . but, given this attention, there need be no fear about results, and in point of durability it will easily prove itself superior to any ordinary brick. For appearance, strength, and durability, the concrete block will be generally preferred to bricks . . . The monolithic form of concrete cottage is also of great interest, especially to urban districts, where there is an abundance of suitable waste material to be had. It has already been proved to be both practicable and economical, and its defects are few and not insuperable.

4. What does the Exhibition teach as to the height of rooms, size of living-room, (minimum) number of bedrooms, etc?

The Exhibition probably teaches that there is one question of more importance than lofty rooms – that is, effective ventilation. The loftier the rooms the more expensive the cottage becomes. It could probably be easily demonstrated that rooms 8 ft. high, with good ventilation, are sufficient for all purposes of health and comfort. Bedrooms, especially in rural districts, might even be a little less lofty than 8 ft. The size and positions of windows, and an arrangement by which they can be opened right to the top, are considerations of very great value.

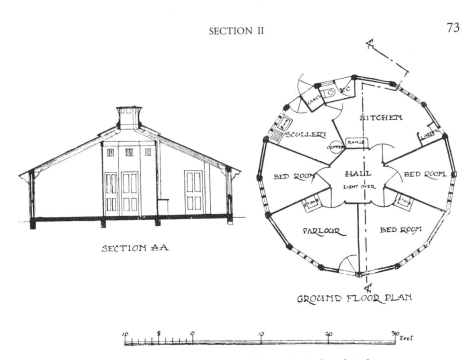

Design for a circular cottage by Messrs Hesketh and Stokes.

A living-room should not be less than 12 ft. sq., which, assuming a height of 8 ft., would make the cubic contents of the room 1152 ft. It is also very important that in all cases a scullery of adequate size should be provided where all the rough housework can be done. If this provision is not made the activities of washing day overflow into the living-room and destroy all sense of order and comfort. This is a matter that is frequently neglected.

5. Is the question of having three bedrooms not somewhat discounted by lodgers being taken in?

The question of the number of bedrooms required is much disputed; and the answer given depends upon the standpoint from which the question is approached. If the physical and moral soundness of the people is the supreme consideration, and in view of the fact that mixed families are the rule in the ordinary course of nature, separate bedrooms for the boys and girls, that is three bedrooms, ought to be provided. But approaching the question from another point of view and taking first into consideration the cost of the cottage and the rent-paying capacity of the labourer, quite an opposite conclusion would be arrived at. Following the usual course of things a cottage with three bedrooms and having other accommodation in proportion involves a capital outlay, and consequently a rent which the ordinary labourer is quite unable to pay. There is scarcely any option but that he shall take in lodgers in order to meet his liabilities.

If the cottage required in the interests of the moral as well as the physical soundness of the labourer and his family is beyond his rent-paying capacity, then it is probably best to forego the third bedroom, exclude the lodger, and give the labourer, at least, the opportunity to foster such privacy as is necessary to a true sense of home life. It is obviously not fair to deny to a large number of people the conditions of decency and then to blame them for their lax morals.

6. Are the baths used to any extent when in the scullery?

Baths are probably used quite as frequently when in the scullery as if they were upstairs. Labouring men and their wives generally are not strongly inclined to frequent bathing . . . They are certainly a bit shy of baths, but opportunity and education may be trusted to accomplish much. In the meantime the children are gradually becoming inured to the process, and in the next generation the prejudice may to some extent be removed.

7. What proportion of cost is added as a result of tiles *versus* slate?

So long as the cost and rent are of such vital importance in fixing the character of the labourer's cottage, this question of tile *versus* slate roofs cannot be lightly dismissed. The substitution of slate for tiles would effect a threefold saving (1) in materials (2) in labour (3) in the strength of the roof timbers. The total saving might be stated at from £6 to £8 per cottage, or in a £150 cottage, a saving of 5% on the gross cost. This may perhaps seem to be only a small saving, but where rigid economy must be observed in every detail this is by no means a negligible amount; many desirable fittings, such as baths and cupboards etc., could be added to a cottage for the same amount.

It is probably erroneous to suppose that the artistic appearance of the cottage depends solely upon a tiled roof! But in any case, the adaptation of the cottage to the needs and means of the labourer is the question of primary importance.

8. What proportion of the cheap cottages are likely to be durable for a 99 years' lease, and what proportion are likely to become subject to heavy repairs after the first year or two?

It is of course a matter of speculation how many cottages will survive until the expiration of the 99 years' lease. Much will depend upon the degree of attention which they receive; but assuming that to be reasonably good, 65% of the cottages may be expected to survive that period of time. In the matter of repairs, it is probable that with the exception of some 30% the owners of the cottages will become involved in costs for repairs after five or six years, and in some cases within an even shorter period of time. There are many causes which will lead to this, where walls are hollow (lath and plaster), roofs imperfect, timbers – especially outside boarding – light in strength; this early and continuous cost in repairs is quite inevitable.

9. Are timber-built cottages quite warm and satisfactory in other respects?

The timber-built, or timber-framed cottages are quite an interesting and instructive part of the Exhibition, and, like the iron-frame cottages have not received the attention which they deserve. Where the framework is sufficiently substantial and the timbers are well-housed together, the exterior covered with good cement, mortar, and rough-cast, and the interior walls well plastered, good results may be reasonably expected in timber-built cottages. If the timber framing inside and out is covered with expanded metal instead of wood laths even better results may be looked for. In any case, for scattered cottages in country districts, and especially in districts where bricks are not easily accessible, this method of cottage-building is worth careful consideration, and will be found to yield quite good results, provided always that the materials and workmanship are sound. Such cottages will be found to be quite comfortable both in winter and summer, and can be built at quite moderate cost.

10. Which cottages have been most sought after by tenants, and for what reasons?

The cottages constructed of brick and concrete blocks have been most sought after, and have found both tenants and purchasers most readily. After these the stronger timber-frame cottages. It must also be stated that a distinct preference has been shown for the cottage with a parlour. These latter were taken up quite promptly, and with only a few exceptions have found purchasers. These cottages are not, however, occupied by what may be properly termed the 'labouring classes', but by people of small means, clerks, etc.

In these different ways the exhibition had brought to light the problems associated with the model cottage. It had demonstrated some of the practical problems which arose through trying to build very cheaply, and illustrated some of the possible new ways found to achieve this. Even if the £150 cottage was not practicable, the exhibition had shown on what basis the model cheap cottage might best be realized:

The approved cottage must combine sound materials, with simplicity of design and construction, and honest workmanship. The exterior must, at least, be sound, proof against all weathers, and neat in appearance; in the interior, the rooms must be sufficient in size, well-lighted, well-ventilated and adequately warmed. Each cottage must be capable of becoming a real home. It is in this way that something may be done to restore the physical soundness, the moral well-being and the simple home-life of that portion of our people who, after all, constitute the very foundation of our national life, and upon whom the health, the wealth, and ultimately the power and the future of this great country rests.

SOURCES

The Architect and Contract Reporter, LXXXIV, 1905, supplement.
British Architect, LXIV, 1905.
Is the cheap cottage a myth? *Garden City*, n.s.I, 1905.

The Standard Cottage, 1916

The notion of the Standard Cottage was promulgated by S.D. Adshead in an article in *Town Planning Review* (Vol. VI, 1916). His appeal for the more controlled and coherent layout of estates was matched by that of many contemporary planners. He directed the attack on a problem that had caused concern since the Model Cottage Exhibition in the early days of the Garden City at Letchworth – that too many little villas can produce a restless effect and, however pretty the individual house, it may have to be modified to bring it into relation with its neighbours.

At the R.I.B.A. Conference on Town Planning in 1910, Raymond Unwin had recognized the need to treat the street as a unit in design terms, rather than simply concentrating on the individual house in its own little garden. In the best of the garden-suburb and village schemes the architects and planners had consciously tried to reconstruct, on the German model, the picturesque street-scheme of the mediaeval town. In many cases, however, they had been content simply to rely on a diversity of housing styles to produce the required informality of appearance. This emphasis on the single house, this lack of unity of perception, was reflected in a restlessness of composition. On those estates where a degree of style had had to be sacrificed to the needs of economy, this was not even compensated for by the intrinsic value of the individual property. As the concept of the garden suburb was adapted to the housing needs of the poorer classes, and as increasing building costs, especially after 1911, necessitated reductions in housing standards, this became an increasing problem for the consideration of planners.

There were, in effect, two alternative methods of simplification. In the first case, the houses could be kept separate, but face upon a road. Simple, rectangular forms would predominate and horizontal lines and flat roofs became common. Patrick Abercrombie urged this use of the 'square house', believing that the composition of the total street picture would compensate for the lack of interest in the isolated house: 'The Square House is able to produce a collective effect by reason of the strongly pronounced horizontality of its line and the very modesty of its design'.

The other method was to have streets of continuous houses, in which case the unity would be of a much higher order. It was of the possibilities of terrace development over again that S.D. Adshead wrote. In this he distinguished the standard house from the process of standardization:

> Standardisation is a very different thing from encasing groups of buildings in an architectural composition, and I am not sure if to standardise is not more degrading than to allow the erection of a heterogeneous collection of distractions which is the extreme in the opposite direction. We can become as wearied with buildings jostling together in

A depraved descendant of the Square House, which a Local Authority is proposing to erect and of which they have asked the Local Government Board to approve.

A caricature of the square house by Patrick Abercrombie.

an architectural confusion as we can become subdued and anaemic with the effects of standardisation. As town planners planning for democracy we should endeavour in public places and in the more closely inhabited areas of a town to introduce a rhythmical continuity or a composition that is symmetrical. It follows, then, the many separate tenements will by the requirements of symmetry need to have their facades exactly repeated, but each will have a definite reference to the whole and, moreover, every habitation – be it cottage, flat or stately mansion – should in one way or another express some sign of the individuality of its inmates.

The model that was being presented here was not then one promoting a particular style or design. It was rather an organizational model. For Adshead the standard cottage was an essential appendage of a highly organized social system, and he argued that without it society could not have that which lay at the very root of national efficiency, organization and economy. He believed that if the war had proved anything, it had proved that national efficiency in the future would depend almost entirely upon good organization:

Organisation is the key note of the success not only of the modern nation, but also of the modern community. Organisation demands the marshalling of individuals having similar interests, and within limits there should follow uniformity in the appearance of their homes.

He recognized, however, that organization could be carried so far as to eliminate entirely the individual, and that standardization of the cottage must, therefore, be limited to community interests, allowing the expression of the individual within these limits. This meant that cottages should be placed on their sites as component parts of a composition, and that this whole should reflect the needs and traditions of the locality and community in which they were placed. Such an approach would require single cottages, semi-detached cottages and rows of cottages as appropriate. Within these different types, there was nevertheless considerable repetition, and what Adshead was arguing for was the saving of labour by mechanically treating much of the material that was to be employed. Repetition and regulation would also induce rapidity in building and precision in allocating materials, and thus there would be a greater saving than there would at first sight appear.

The Standard Cottage utilized labour-saving contrivances and machine-made materials to the full. To this end Adshead advocated that for the construction of the walls it was unlikely that anything would be found more suitable or cheaper than concrete or brick. For strength, in order to keep out the wet, outside walls should normally be 9 in thick, but if reinforced, this thickness could be reduced by half and sufficient strength retained; 4½ in walls of brick or smooth concrete slabs would not of themselves keep out the damp and, therefore, there was always the need for cavity. Adshead recognized that there was no quick and easy way to cut down on the cost of construction, and considered that it was best to construct the outside walls of cottages of brick or concrete, and occasionally of stone, according to what proved cheaper in different localities.

This did not mean that he was not interested in the employment of new materials in the construction of the Standard Cottage. There was scope for embodying in the design of such cottages and incorporating within their traditional character such new materials as roofing felt, asbestone and sheet-iron covered with lead. At the same time, walls could be strengthened horizontally by the assistance of wire, and vertically by the introduction of a light steel frame to carry the roof. The walls themselves could be made warmer by applying on their inner surface thin breeze slabs. Inside partitions could be made of 2 in coke-breeze slabs up to the first floor, and all that the walls would then require would be a thin skim of plaster. Such a system of construction, Adshead argued, would be extremely economical if a big repetition was involved and was combined with standardization as regards doors, skirtings, cupboards, staircases, ranges, baths etc.

The essential condition of the plan and elevation of a Standard Cottage, however, was that it should be elemental and simple in form:

> Here there is no room for corners, no room for features that only lean against the mass, and perhaps most important of all, no room for detail of peculiar interest: detail which might be a pleasure to look at once but which continually repeated would be like the constant repetition of an irritating catch-phrase.

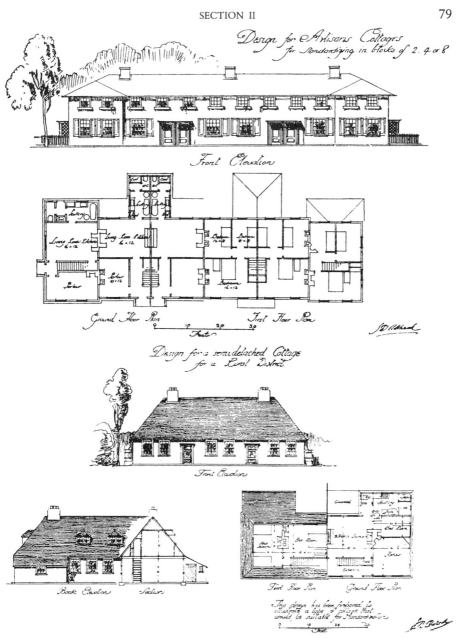

Two of S.D. Adshead's designs for standard cottages.

Two illustrations of cottages which Adshead considered suitable for standardiza-tion are reproduced here. The assumed requirements are a five-roomed semi-detached cottage for a rural district, where a wide frontage is obtainable; and a five-roomed cottage with a 17 ft frontage suitable for erection in groups.

Cottages such as these might in conjunction with one or two others of a different design be erected in thousands with an occasional specially designed cottage on a special site. Ten-thousand sash windows, two-thousand front doors, one-thousand staircases, baths, coppers and stoves, with a machine for turning out a million concrete slabs, each numbered to fill a place, would certainly effect an enormous reduction in cost. It would be well if, with all the cottages that it is absolutely essential that we build in the near future, those responsible for their erection gave consideration to the adoption of standard designs.

The opportunity for realizing the notion for the Standard Cottage came in the war time schemes of the Ministry of Munitions at Gretna and Dormanstown. There the cottages were built with the proportions, repetition and simplicity of the neo-Georgian style which was being advocated by Professor Reilly and the Liverpool School of Architects, who were so critical of the romanticism of the Garden City and its architecture of 'gables, oak-beams, ingle-nooks and bob-and-string latches'. During the war the aesthetic arguments were reinforced by the requirements for speedy production and the demands for efficiency. As a result, 'by the time of the armistice, "simplification, standardization" had acquired all the force of popular orthodoxy'.

SOURCES

Abercrombie, P. (1913) The square house. *Town Planning Review*, **IV**.

Adshead, S.D. (1916) The standard cottage. *Town Planning Review*, **VI**.

Budden, L.B. (1916) The standardisation of elements of design in domestic architecture. *Town Planning Review*, **VI**.

Pepper, S. & Swenarton, M. (1980) Neo-Georgian maison-type: the Liverpool School and the architecture of mass housing. *Architectural Review*, **CLXVII**.

Ramsey, S.C. (1916) The small house of a hundred years ago. *Town Planning Review*, **VI**.

Local Government Board Manual for State-Aided Housing Schemes, 1919

The shortage of working class housing accommodation is one of the most serious problems with which the country is faced at the conclusion of the war . . . The present problem differs from the pre-war problem not only in degree but in kind. The shortage has affected the houses of all classes of working people and is not confined to those poorer classes, with whose housing local authorities have hitherto chiefly been concerned. The standard of accommodation and equipment demanded in their houses by all sections of the working people has been rising . . . The Board are of the opinion, therefore, that the most serious shortage is of good houses, adequate in size, equipment and amenity to afford satisfactory dwellings for a working man's family . . .

The opening statement of the Local Government Board Manual reflects the view that in the immediate post-war period the quality of housing was as important as its quantity, and demonstrates the extent to which post-war housing was no longer conceived of in terms of pre-war types. The standards for new development had been set down in the Tudor Walters Report, which covered four main areas: housing policy and administration; the layout of housing schemes; the standard of accommodation in the houses themselves; the cost of housing. This was a radical programme and nowhere was its impact clearer than with reference to housing standards. The Report turned accepted housing policy on its head, for as Mark Swenarton has demonstrated, Tudor Walters argued that good economy actually demanded major improvements in housing standards.

These standards were ultimately reflected in the Local Government Board Manual, which was in accord with the principles of the Tudor Walters Report, and which was intended as a guide to local authorities on the layout, design and control of housing schemes:

i. In designing house plans a consideration of the first importance is the matter of aspect, and a uniform plan should not be adopted for different aspects. (Plans were included in the manual for general guidance.)

ii. Adequate frontage, generally of not less than 20 ft., should be given to the buildings to allow convenient planning, good lighting of all the parts and any avoidance of back projections.

iii. Good exterior design in harmony with the surroundings and adapted to the site should be secured; on sites of varying character each individual group of buildings will need to be carefully adapted to a suited position and to take advantage of opportunities

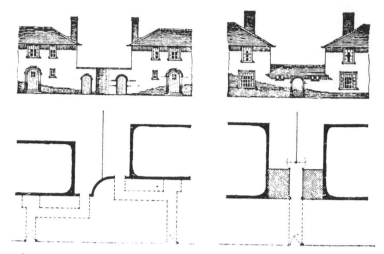

Diagram showing the use of walls and outbuildings to link houses and create a unity of appearance.

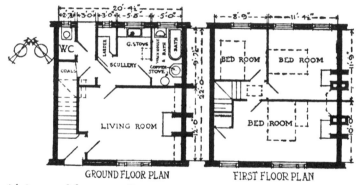

House with increased frontage, allowing separation of bath from scullery, and allocation of greater space to living-room and bedrooms.

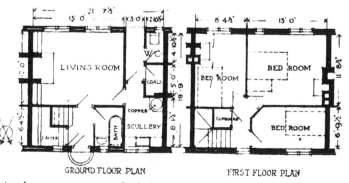

House giving better opportunity for lighting and ventilating throughout all parts of the house.

as to aspect, prospect and levels which that position offers. By the choice of suitable local materials, and the adoption of simple lines and good proportion and grouping of the buildings, with well considered variation in design and in the treatment of prominent parts, good appearance may be secured within the limits required by due economy.

iv. It will suffice here to summarise the general requirements which the Board consider should be met.

(a) The self-contained two-storey cottage type should generally be adopted.

(b) Each house should ordinarily include the following accommodation: living room, scullery, larder, fuel store, wc, bath in separate chamber, and three bedrooms.

(c) Most schemes should include a considerable proportion of houses having parlours and also a certain number of houses having more than three bedrooms. In some cases it may be desirable to include a proportion of houses with only two bedrooms.

v. The living room should be arranged with as few doors as practicable, which should be placed so that they will not interfere with the comfort and convenience of those occupying the space about window and fire. The cooking range, whether in this room or the scullery, should be placed on a wall at right angles to a window wall. The best aspect for the living room is south east, and it must never have a northerly aspect except when sunlight can be admitted at the other end of the room.

vi. The parlour should be planned to leave comfortable space around fire and window. The best aspect is a westerly one. Preference should, however, be given to the living room in this matter of aspect.

vii. The scullery, especially, depends for convenience on arrangement as well as size, and, when it is to be used as a place for cooking, should be provided with the necessary space for small table and cupboard. While sufficient space should be given for convenience it is not desirable to encourage the use of the scullery as a living room. The sink should be placed under or near the window, which should preferably overlook the garden. The copper should be fitted with a steam outlet. A suitable area outside the back door of the house should generally be paved with cement or other impervious material.

viii. The bath, should, where practicable, be in a separate compartment.

ix. Hot water should generally be provided to the sink and to the bath.

x. The larder should be on the northerly side of the house. Where this is impractical the window should be screened from the sun.

xi. The coal store should generally be so placed that coal may be delivered from outside, and fetched for use under cover.

xii. A wc should be accessible under cover. In larger houses it may be on the first floor. Where there is an earth-closet it must be constructed outside the house.

xiii. The stairs should usually start from the entrance lobby, and a window to open should be provided to light and ventilate the landing.

xiv. The bedrooms should be placed as far as possible on the more sunny side of the house; two at least should have fireplaces, and adequate ventilation should be provided

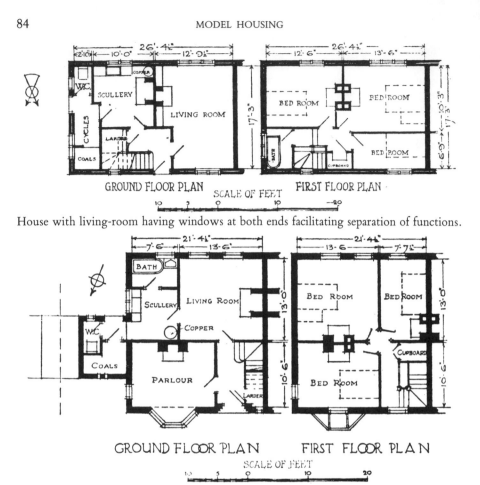

House with living-room having windows at both ends facilitating separation of functions.

Semi-detached parlour house with projections for offices allowing necessary extended accommodation under the main roof.

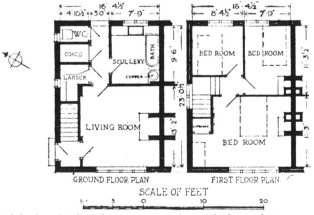

Small house with bath in kitchen, living-room and main bedroom having southerly aspect.

for any not having fireplaces. In every bedroom there should be one window of which the top is at least 6 ft. 6 in. from the floor. If sloping ceilings are adopted, proper headroom must be provided for furniture.

xv. Projections or detached out-buildings for coal and wc should generally be avoided in urban or suburban areas.

xvi. Economy must be secured in every possible way. Among other means it may be obtained by adopting simple planning and design; by placing those parts of the house requiring plumbing and drainage services as near as possible together; by grouping the flues into as few chimney stacks as possible; by adopting a reasonable height for the rooms, say 8 ft.; and by avoiding needless exterior works requiring periodical painting, such as bargeboards, fascias, and imitation timber. It should not, however, be secured by cutting down unduly the size of the rooms, and should not be attempted by adopting other than sound methods of construction.

Following through these criteria, attention was attached to the question of the number of houses to be erected to the acre. Great importance was given to the provision of an adequate area of land in connection with state-aided housing schemes, so that sufficient gardens, allotments, playgrounds, grass or other open space might be arranged. To provide for this, the Board considered that each house should have the equivalent of 400 yd^2 of land, which would result in a density of twelve houses to the acre 'gross area' in urban areas, and eight houses to the acre 'net area' in rural areas.

At the same time it was recommended that capable architects should be employed to plan and design the houses, in order to ensure economy in plans and simplicity in design. It was stressed that economy in maintenance should be considered in conjunction with capital costs, and that all materials employed should be of a durable kind and of good quality. To this end, detailed specifications were provided for brick walls, stone walls, other construction materials, roofs, partitions, floors, staircases and services.

Finally, note was taken of the needs of site-planning in relation to houses, though limited attention was given to this aspect of the model. The Manual simply stated:

> The greatest economy in lay-out will depend on full advantage being taken of all the opportunities which the site affords. The location of different parts of the scheme should first be determined, and reservations made for open spaces, shops and other buildings serving a beneficial purpose in the scheme; these being grouped where possible to form a centre. The lay-out should, in addition to satisfying the utilitarian requirements, develop the order and individual character of a good design. By so planning the lines of the roads and disposing the spaces and the buildings as to develop the beauty of vista, arrangement and proportion, attractiveness may be added to the dwellings at little or no extra cost.

The implications of the model promulgated by the Local Government Board have been summarized by Swenarton:

> . . . by the middle of 1919 the Tudor Walters Report was accepted as a quasi-official

statement of the Government's housing policy. At the core of the report was the notion that economy could be secured by the expertise of the designer. By flexible planning, by the code of simplification and by the various techniques known to the experienced designer . . . considerable savings could be achieved and a substantial improvement in the standards of housing could be made without a corresponding increase in capital out-lay. Whereas in the past it had appeared that the lowering of housing standards was the only route to economy, the Tudor Walters Report suggested that these savings could be achieved by expertise in design.

SOURCES

Local Government Board (1918) *Report of Committee on Building Construction in connection with the Provision of Dwellings for the Working Classes in England, Wales and Scotland.*

Local Government Board (1919) *Manual on the Preparation of State-aided Housing Schemes.*

Swenarton, M. (1981) *Homes Fit for Heroes.* London: Heinemann.

The Residential Area, 1927

Even in its purely physical aspect, a home is more than a house; it is, in part, a creature of certain external qualities in its surroundings. It may, for example, be well designed, have solid walls and good sanitation, and yet be a most defective house because of the presence in its neighbourhood of ugly structures, congested streets and yards and untidy open spaces, and noxious use of buildings.

Thus Thomas Adams characterized the broader environmental concerns of housing in the mid-1930s. A realization that housing reform was not just a matter of the individual house had been inherent in the Garden City and Town Planning Movement from the outset. As development progressed after the First World War, it was increasingly recognized that it was not primarily in the design of the cottages themselves, but in the relation of the cottages to each other, that most mistakes of layout had occured. When the Ministry of Health issued its *Housing Manual on the Design, Construction and Repair of Dwellings* in 1927, therefore, it devoted a major section to the question of site-planning, and provided guidelines for the layout of the model residential area. This was putting into practice the broad principles of what was commonly referred to as the Garden City type of development.

Probably the most general improvement in housing since the war is to be noticed in the arrangement or layout of the sites, the reduced density of the dwellings, and the provision of open spaces in connection with them. A few considerations are, however, sufficiently often neglected to call for mention.

1. The low altitude to which the sun rises in this country during the winter months, when its rays have a special scarcity value, is not always recognised. In mid-winter that altitude is only about 15° above the horizon at noon; and an obstruction showing an altitude of 45° from any window having a south aspect will exclude all direct sunshine for about six months of the year. It is very important when laying out the roads or spacing the buildings, particularly where blocks of flats or other high erections are concerned, to arrange that ample sunshine has access to the windows of all living rooms.

2. That back roads are unsuitable for open development and needlessly add to first costs and maintenance charges, is still not fully realised. With the length of garden usually provided such roads are too far from the house to be convenient, and considerable lengths have to be made to join up to the front road. When houses are built in pairs no difficulty arises as to secondary access. When built in groups of four or more several alternative methods may be adopted. On the whole the passage through the block, when allowance is made for the valuable extra space afforded for bedrooms, is probably in the long run the most economical and convenient.

87

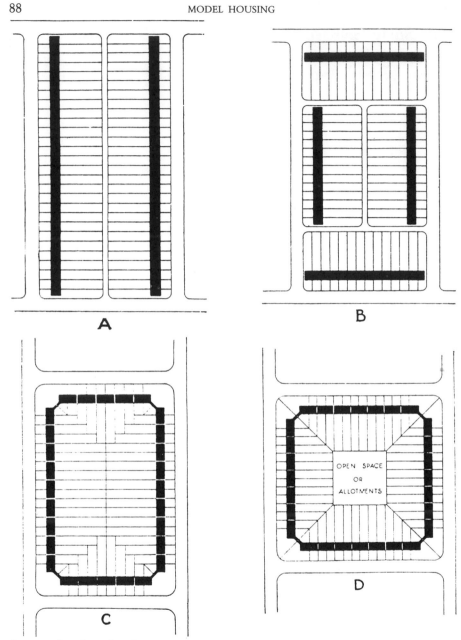

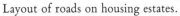

Layout of roads on housing estates.

A and B: Two arrangements of development with back roads, showing the inconvenience when used with gardens.

C and D: Two arrangements providing on similar areas of land equal numbers of houses of like frontage without back roads, secondary access being arranged between each pair of houses.

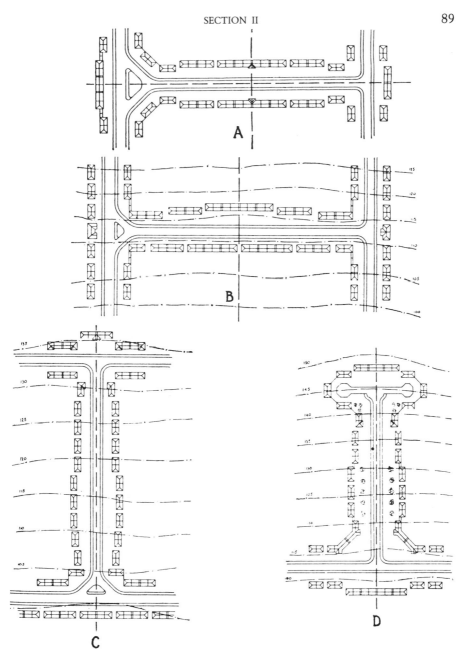

Grouping of houses, illustrating the necessity of taking count of the contours of the ground.

A: For level site: groups may balance about either or both centre lines.

B: For slope across the road; the only satisfactory balance is about the transverse axis.

C and D: For slopes in the direction of roads which allow balance about longitudinal axis only.

3. Cases of density higher than the normal are sometimes put forward in connection with the laying out of new sites where an examination of the relative cost per house of development in each case would show that the small saving which the increased density would effect in the cost of land is counter-balanced by the increase in road and sewer costs needed to provide available frontage for the extra houses. It is seldom that road costs per house are not increased by increased density, and frequently the increase is substantial. If a comparison of these figures with the relative size and value of the resulting plots in each case were made, frequently it would be evident that the increase in density, instead of resulting in any saving for the purchaser or tenant of the house, results only in his paying substantially the same price or rent for a very inferior plot, affording much curtailed garden ground and less ample air space. Only where land reaches a price higher than is usually given for cottage building sites is any economy to be effected by an increase in density.

4. To secure the full economic advantage and the improved amenity of reduced density, only sufficient length of road should be constructed to provide adequate frontage for the houses to be built. Full advantage should also be taken of the opportunities afforded by more open development for so arranging the roads in relation to the contours that the construction of the roads and the foundations of the buildings will be economical, and the placing and grouping of the buildings will be advantageous in regard to aspect and pleasing in appearance.

5. Owing to the loss of frontage at road junctions needless crossroads should be avoided. Development by short open cul-de-sac roads is economical where such treatment is suitable; and as a means of removing dwellings from fronting directly upon heavy traffic roads, they may be useful. For like reasons of economy acute angled junctions should be avoided where they are not required to meet definite traffic convenience.

6. Where land has a slope greater than one in ten special arrangements in regard to layout are called for in order to keep the cost of house foundations within reasonable bounds. Sometimes narrow roads having houses on the high side only will prove of advantage in such cases.

7. In regard to the minor development roads which do not carry through traffic, some reduction in the width and character of construction is reasonable and economical. It is not always realised that the saving of future maintenance charges at a capital cost the interest on which exceeds those charges can hardly be regarded as justified on grounds of economy.

8. Frontage is sometimes wasted in a quite unnecessary effort to make all the gardens exactly the same size, even where they come against a road junction or corner. Such an arrangement is unsuitable to open development; by it the backs of the houses are unduly exposed, and a ragged appearance is given to the street junctions.

9. The total length of frontage on the layout plan should be compared with that actually occupied by the buildings as a check on the economy of the scheme.

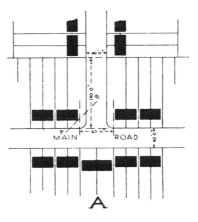

A

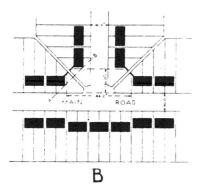

B

C

Street junctions. Diagrams showing alternative arrangements of houses and the loss of road frontage involved in each case. The line AB in each shows the amount of clear vision for traffic.

Light road or drive round green as means of road economy. With contours as shown in the sketch further economy in building would be effected by the arrangement.

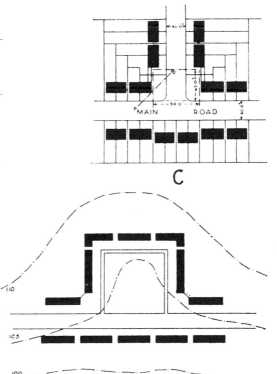

10. While it is important to avoid the first cost and maintenance of a needless extent of road surfaces, by avoiding too many crossroads, or uneconomical junctions; it is equally necessary for economy in the building not to curtail the frontage provided for the buildings below the length which will allow for good and economical planning. The sum saved by unduly curtailing such frontage may be exceeded considerably by the extra cost to projections, out-buildings, or other such expedients.

11. Much of the effect of the layout design depends on the careful and orderly planning of road bends and junctions, and on the placing and treatment of the houses adjacent to them. In all cases where the end elevations are exposed at corners the houses should be properly designed to provide for the two faces being seen together. Unless specially adapted to the position, houses placed diagonally across a corner do not usually look well. Even when suitably designed, they are seldom pleasing unless well set back behind the building lines of the streets. At important corners specially designed groups may be used to turn the angle; otherwise the corners may be made satisfactory by bridging the ends of the two rows of houses fairly near to each other and filling the diagonal space with a wall, out-building, or with screen of hedge or shrubs.

12. Design of a group of houses may be good in itself and the materials appropriate to the locality, and yet the building may not be adapted to its particular site, or it may be uncomfortably placed on the ground. On sloping or sharply undulating land it is of particular importance to arrange the groups so that they will sit well on the site. Buildings set diagonally with the plane of slope seldom look well; and the defect is not easily remedied by terracing the ground. Generally buildings are most satisfactory when arranged with their longer face parallel with the contour lines and the shallower depth at right angles to them.

13. If the outline of a mass of a building by reason of gable, chimney, sloping roof or out-building has a higher and a lower side or end, it will generally look better and firmer on its site if the higher part of the building stands on the lower part of the slope.

14. Much may be done by the careful arrangement of the buildings to introduce pleasing relationship and orderly grouping, the true variety; the very opposite, be it noted, of mere change for the sake of change. To break away from the straight line by scattering the units in a random irregularity is but to destroy the chief virtue which the long straight row has, namely, its orderliness, without producing any new relation to take its place.

15. An orderly grouping does not necessarily mean one that is symmetrical on plan. On undulating sites it is important to remember that symmetry demands balance in levels as well as on plan; and where this cannot be secured some other grouping will usually be desirable.

16. Irregularities in the site, fine existing trees or other features to be preserved, will suggest many opportunities for varied grouping, which may be as important for economy in foundations as for variety in appearance. Difference in aspect of the various sites will demand a change of plan to secure the proper share of sunlight for the living-rooms, shade for the larder, or shelter for the doors of the house.

These are some reasons for introducing variation in the arrangement or in the type and treatment of the buildings. If advantage is taken of them there will generally be sufficient change to relieve tendency to monotony; and the variation will arise in a pleasing and natural manner very different from the crude expedients frequently adopted, such as altering the position or treatment of alternate groups of houses, slating one, tiling another, facing one with brick or plastering another, without reason, merely for the sake of change.

These guidelines, incorporating advice with regard to both site-planning and roads, reflect the views of the producing agency as distinct from the consumer. As against the standardized semi-detached housing type, the Manual demonstrated how a close group of dwellings in terrace-formation, in streets, squares and crescents, might, without sacrificing low density, not only allow of more effective provision of communal facilities in the form of greens, gardens and open spaces, but might also be more conducive to the creation of a stronger sense of civic pride than could arise from a scattered form of development. Such residential concerns place the interests of the community before those of the individual.

SOURCES

Adams, T. (1934) *The Design of Residential Areas: Basic Considerations, Principles and Methods.* Cambridge, Mass.: Harvard University Press.

Ministry of Health (1927) *Housing Manual on the Design, Construction and Repair of Dwellings.*

A National Housing Policy, 1934

In 1934 a National Housing Committee was formed by a small group of eminent people representing architectural, social, political and religious interests. Their purpose was to examine the vital problem of national housing and to submit proposals that would be of assistance to the Government. The Committee's prime consideration was that action should be co-ordinated and not of a piecemeal character, and its report, of the same year, tackled the question of how to deal with the problem of the provision of housing accommodation, not below a minimum standard, for every family in the United Kingdom at a rent within the family's capacity to pay. Fit and proper housing, the Committee argued, was a national essential, in the absence of which other social legislation would be ineffective. The 1930 Housing Act had placed on local authorities the statutory obligation to provide housing and prepare proposals. The Committee brought forward its report with the intention that it should embody the general principles most likely to bring success. As the Committee concluded, 'We know of no alternative approach which has the remotest chance of doing so'.

Given these principles, the Committee was unequivocal in its response to the minimum standard of decent housing accommodation: 'The answer which all practical men have given is that we want the three-bedroomed non-parlour house with a 760 sq ft area, which can be let within the means of the lower-paid wage-earner . . .'.

The Committee accepted the 760 ft^2 as a fair estimate, though it was prepared to admit that the figure might have to be raised if the general standard of living rose. Also, apart from this problem of family accommodation, suitable provision would have to be made among the dwellings for those without children and others whose needs were on a lesser scale, for example, aged people and pensioners.

The Committee was concerned that these reasonable requirements should be satisfied at costs within the means of the lower-paid worker. It therefore, secondly, addressed the question of rents. Careful examination of family budgets of lower-paid workers indicated that householders having dependants, and whose incomes did not exceed 50 s. a week, could not rightly afford more than 10 s. a week for rent and rates. Since the weekly earnings of a very large proportion of the workers in the country did not exceed 50 s., the problem before the Committee was to provide houses to let at 10 s. a week and under. The Ministry of Health had put forward as a desirable object a rent of 10 s. a week (inclusive of rates) or less, and the Committee pointed out that this also must cover interest and sinking-funds, insurance, repairs, maintenance, management and rates.

In these circumstances the Committee stressed that the houses required were ones to let and not for sale. The arguments for encouraging those with assured employment and good pay to purchase their homes outright did not apply to the majority of low-paid or migrating workers. Irregularities of employment often prevented the low-wage earner from keeping up instalments, while the commitment to buy his own house tied him down to one area and did not leave him free to follow up opportunities of finding work elsewhere. His risks were high in comparison with his wage expectations, and if he was in financial difficulties he would be unable to keep his property in repair, and would probably be forced to sub-let or take in lodgers, thus providing the nucleus of a new slum.

To meet these requirements the Committee adopted the approach advocated by the Ministry of Health's *Housing Manual on the Design, Construction and Repair of Dwellings* published in 1927. This had been based on the view that economy was not an obstacle to the erection of pleasant dwellings, nor in itself a reason for adopting bad designs and inappropriate treatment:

> In the building of new houses simple forms and appropriate materials will count for much; and the general uniformity which may be demanded by economy can be relieved at a cost which is almost negligible, if, instead of spoiling the simplicity of all the houses with cheap-looking bays, door heads or other features, an occasional touch of emphasis and variety is secured by a well designed and carefully placed feature to mark the centre of a group, the termination of a street vista, or the turning of a corner.

In pursuit of this policy the standards originally proposed were perforce lowered as a result of the restrictions of the Housing Act of 1930. The impact of this on room areas and heights, and planning of facilities was seen in the Manual of 'typical plans' published by the Ministry of Health in 1933. However, despite their limitations, these models still followed the expectations incorporated in the 1927 Manual which formed the basis of the National Housing Policy of 1934. These were expressed in relation to the different rooms and functions of the houses:

> *Living room.* In this room all the occupants habitually assemble, and in it the family life has to be carried on. Sufficient space for the purpose, plenty of light and sunshine, and convenience of arrangement to meet the many needs are essential. It should be given preference in the matter of aspect with the object of securing as much sunshine as the conditions of the site allow, and affording as cheerful an outlook as possible from the windows. It should be planned so that the spaces about the windows and fire, where the occupants will naturally wish to sit and work or rest, will be as free as possible from disturbing cross traffic from door to door . . . This plan of living room involves a house of longer frontage and shallower depth than usual . . . This plan also lends itself to the production of a better proportioned building where houses are erected in pairs. The narrower roof span, with resulting reduction in height of gable or party walls and chimneys, frequently compensates in cost for the increased length of outside wall required to contain a given area in oblong shape as compared with a shape more nearly square.

> *Bedrooms.* The main considerations in the planning of bedrooms are that spaces in size and shape convenient for the beds and for the necessary furniture should be provided.

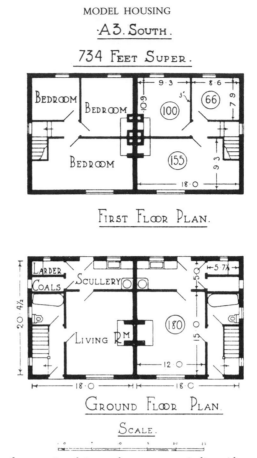

·A3. South.

734 Feet Super.

First Floor Plan.

Ground Floor Plan.

Scale.

House with short frontage involving rather narrow window side to living-room, but economical bedroom plan.

Windows should be so placed that they can conveniently be opened, and the fireplaces planned so that they can be used without inconvenience. Sash windows or casements should be hung so that parts can be opened in rainy weather in order to secure constant ventilation. The great value of flues for ventilation should be remembered . . . Sunshine is important to sweeten the rooms during the day and in case of sickness. Rooms with only north aspects should be avoided where practicable.

Scullery. Health, cleanliness, and convenience alike demand the provision of a small scullery or wash-house to relieve the living room from wet and dirty work. Without such a room it is almost impossible to keep the living room in a reasonably fit condition for its purpose. There is a serious objection to the type of dwelling in which the sink is placed in the living room and a parlour is provided in place of a scullery. The parlour may afford a refuge from the living room when its condition is rendered too unsatisfactory, but it does nothing to keep the living room free from the dirt, damp, or unpleasant odours inseparable from many of the processes which should be relegated to a

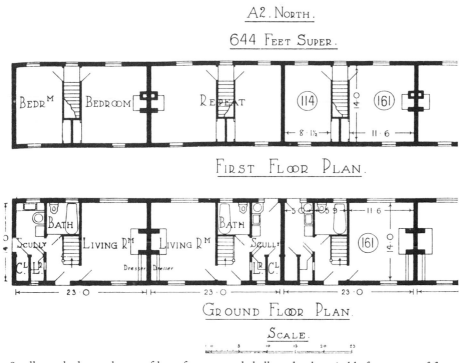

A2. North.

644 Feet Super.

First Floor Plan.

Ground Floor Plan.

Scale.

Small two-bedroom house of long frontage and shallow depth, suitable for groups of four or six.

scullery . . . The main considerations affecting the planning of sculleries are: space for the sink and draining boards, under or immediately adjacent to the window; space for the copper so placed that anyone standing at the sink will not be in danger from the fire; space for mangle if in general use, and for the necessary utensils.

Bathroom. The bathroom will, with advantage, be placed on the ground floor; and in the case of houses having one living room only, with three bedrooms on the first floor, the area of these, with the landing for access, will cover space on the ground floor suffi-cient to provide a bathroom there. Considerable extra area on both floors must be pro-vided in this type of house to enable the bathroom to be placed upstairs. Such space would, of course, add greatly to the convenience of living rooms, scullery, etc, and may be very desirable; but where the minimum costs consistent with the provision of essentials is aimed at, the bathroom should be planned downstairs. It is more conve-nient as bathroom when accessible direct from the stairs, but may serve more readily as wash-house if placed adjacent to the scullery; economy in plumbing and drainage may also suggest this position.

Larder. The larder is an essential. It should be on the north side or be carefully shielded from the hot sun. Good light and ample ventilation to an outside area which is free from risk of contamination are important.

Parlour. The advantage of a second small sitting room needs no explanation. This room is, however, placed last in order of importance because, valuable as it may be, the parlour is not so necessary for healthy and decent family life as the other rooms and accessories mentioned. As a rule, therefore, it should only be included in the family dwelling when it can be given in addition to the other accommodation and not instead of it. Where a parlour is provided, the living room does not serve quite so many functions and can, therefore, be reduced a little in size . . . Many of the purposes for which a parlour is valuable can be served by quite a small room; little more, in fact, than a recess opening from the living room will do much to provide the needed retirement for reading, writing, dressmaking and other occupations with which the general movement in the living room is liable to interfere. While, therefore, a fair-sized parlour is desirable, the benefit of quite a small room is not one to be despised.

These principles were set forth in the Housing Manual as being those which would provide the types of accommodation and layout which would be most suitable to the working classes. This was clearly a model to be handed down, though it was at least recognized that prospective tenants might have their own views as to their housing interests:

Dwellings should be carefully designed to suit the manner of life of the people for whom they are intended, and to encourage or forestall any improvements in that manner which health, cleanliness, or improved standards of education are likely to call for.

Adopting this approach, the National Housing Committee reinforced the continuing demand for house-building and the need for housing reform, and urged the need for the efforts of both private enterprise and public authorities to be co-ordinated and not to be of a piecemeal character. It turned the housing policy and expectations of the government into a 'crusade'; a model was thus prescribed on a scale not hitherto contemplated.

SOURCES

Ministry of Health (1927) *Housing Manual on the Design, Construction and Repair of Dwellings.*
National Housing Committee (1934) *A National Housing Policy.*

Kensal House,
an Urban Village, 1936

Kensal House, characterized as the first 'urban village' in England, was an experiment in re-housing families from slum areas, carried out by the Gas Light and Coke Company. The scheme arose from the appointment of a committee of architects (Robert Atkinson, Maxwell Fry, C.H. James, Grey Wornum) and a housing consultant (Elizabeth Denby) to consider the kind of equipment most suitable for working class homes. But the availability of a redundant site, along with a sense of public utility, led the company to the idea of installing the equipment in actual dwellings.

Later, it was decided that the estate should be developed in strict accordance with the terms of the 1930 Slum Clearance and Re-Housing Act and in co-operation with Kensington Borough Council as part of its rehousing programme. In these circumstances the development committee was required: '. . . to comply with national and local regulations and requirements, to design an estate suitable for a comparatively mixed but poor population, with large families, and to see that the weekly outgoings on fuel and light were as reasonable as the rent'.

Here architects were to put into practice the notion of the house as a machine for living in. Following the precepts of modern architecture, the 'house' was to be built from within, with the emphasis on the purpose of the building, the organization of the plan and the ordering of masses on a large scale; beauty was not to arise from ornament, but rather from sensitivity to the proportions and harmonies of planes and surfaces, and from the art involved in areas and angles, textures and weight, light and shade. At the same time, consideration of cost necessitated a design and form of construction which lent itself to repetition and standardization. The task of the architects was '. . . to mould these standardised units into good architectural groups, well gardened and planted, and to avoid the barren barrack appearance of the earlier tenement buildings'.

At Kensal House, mass production was utilized through a type-plan in which design concentrated on the model unit, which could then be combined and co ordinated in relation to the needs of the whole scheme. With slight variations there was one type-plan, appearing in its purest form as a three-bedroomed flat, with living-room and balcony, and a working unit consisting of kitchen, drying-balcony opening off it, and bathroom next door. On the ground floors and curved parts of the blocks, this plan was modified to provide a two-bedroomed flat. Maxwell Fry identified the benefits of this design:

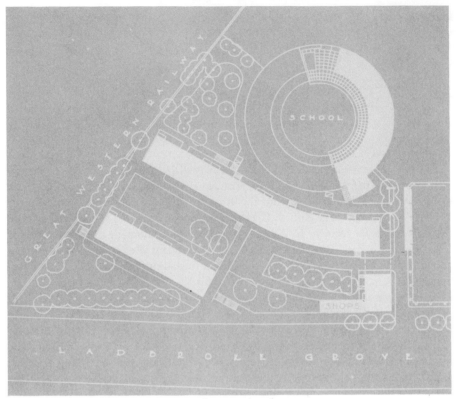

Kensal House site plan.

The standard flat plan was largely governed by an early decision to have internal stair-case access instead of outside galleries, which are un-private, draughty, barrack like and loved by nobody. With internal staircases there is greater privacy, and a nice feeling of going up your own staircase, the staircase is under cover, has its own front door and is more civilised for these things. In addition, it allows all bedrooms to be on one side of the flat, which makes it easier to design good bedrooms and a workable flat. Here also, by planning the blocks to run north and south, it allows the morning sun to aerate the bedrooms and, later in the day, to warm and cheer the living quarters. That is the basis of the flat.

The result of planning to meet tenants' needs and wishes was the amount of space given to the living-room at the expense of bedrooms. At the same time the kitchen was also made small, with the idea that, if it were made really workable without being cramped, and if it were equipped with good fittings not too costly to run, then it could be used for work only, and meals would be taken in the living-room. It was the kitchen, which along with the bathroom formed the 'working unit', that received the greatest attention, partly for the reasons given and partly because of the interests of the promoters. It was designed as a model to be tested for workability.

Model kitchen, Kensal House.

Thus the kitchen was laid out with the sink and draining-boards on one side, and shelves, worktables and cupboards on the other, so that there was maximum space free for work and a proper provision of direct light. The bathroom was next to the kitchen, with the bath and washbasin arranged so that all pipes could run between the kitchen and bathroom walls, with a common gas-heater serving both. The large living-room opened out onto the balcony, which was designed not to overshadow the whole room. For heating the company provided coke stoves and gas fires. The dimensions of the rooms in this basic model were: living room 185 ft² bedrooms, 125, 98, 72 ft² respectively; kitchen 96 ft².

This type of flat was repeated to make up the development, which comprised sixty-eight flats in three blocks with fifty-four four-room flats and fourteen three-room flats. With fifty-one dwellings to the acre, this housing was designed to meet the needs of 380 persons on one and a third acres, while at the same time '. . . trying to preserve beauty and secure serenity and privacy in the homelife of the tenants'.

In addition to the flats, the development provided adult and juvenile club-rooms, a nursery school for sixty children, a playground, a quiet space and allotments. With these facilities, the estate allowed the opportunity to experiment in community organization and control, not only through the different amenities but also through the management and rent collection. Tenants were encouraged to take up gardening and thereby bring an expression of individuality to each balcony and to the estate as a whole. The response reflected the continuing search for *rus in urbe*:

General view of Kensal House.

On a sunny evening or at the weekend each balcony has its tenants leaning elbows on the rail, smoking, gossiping, happy, like a group of cottagers perched above each other on a steep cliff. The possession of canarys by some of the tenants intensifies the country illusion.

Kensal House thus illustrated two complementary approaches to housing: the social and the technical. The developers recognized that the validity of their model depended on the extent to which technical advances contributed to the quality of life of the tenants. The scheme was animated by the desire to build a group of houses where people whose incomes allowed them little above sheer necessity could experience as full a life as possible. It was recognized that the essentials to such a life lay in the house itself, since in the slums from which the tenants came, hardship centred about the lack of practical things, such as space, sun, air, hot water, cooking facilities and so on. The provision of such facilities was prominent in the design process in order that their lack could be remedied within the inevitable financial constraints. The consequences were estimated in both physical and moral terms:

These tenants are poor, many of them really poor – that is to say they have about 3s. 6d. to 6s. a head left for food and clothing after they have paid rents and outgoings. But they are aglow with pride at their new homes and their responsibility for managing them. Most of them are actually paying less than they were in their bad old rooms, and every week sees some new adornment added to the nest. The tenants of Kensal House are a fine example of the latent potentiality in every slum-dweller which only needs freeing from weeds before they flower.

This model of what could be achieved in a self-contained estate, with its own range of amenities, both reflected what was being done at the same time by some of the more progressive local authorities, and also set standards for dwellings that were to come into more general circulation. Though the momentum of the Modern Movement for flat dwellings was not maintained through the 1930s, such models as this typified the transition that had taken place from working class tenement to modern flat, and demonstrated the possible high levels of privacy and comfort which good design could achieve.

SOURCES

Ascot Gas Water Heaters (1938) *Flats, Municipal and Private Enterprise*. London: Ascot Gas Water Heaters Ltd.

Bertram, C.A.G. (1935) *The House, A Machine for Living In*. London: Black.

The People's Model:
A Mass Observation Survey, 1943

The Second World War, through enemy destruction and the forced interruption of the housing cycle, brought with it a housing shortage of dimensions never known before. Architects and planners were involved in arguments about what sort of housing to build, small or large, whether one or two sitting-rooms, two or three bedrooms, whether to build them in the middle of towns, in suburbs, or in whole new communities. It was recognized, perhaps for the first time, that they would have to take into account the needs and wishes of the people for whom they were going to build new homes. The government acknowledged this fact by appointing a special sub-committee of the Ministry of Health Central Housing Committee, under the chairmanship of Lord Dudley, to enquire into the design of houses and flats in post-war building. At the same time, there were many bodies, particularly women's organizations, active in the process of discovering housing preferences.

The problem with much of this activity was that the questions were quite unscientifically framed, and were likely to raise demands artificially. It was for this reason that the Mass Observation Unit, which had been documenting the processes of social change since 1938, undertook its enquiry, which aimed at a broader picture with the minimum of pre-supposition:

> We are not here concerned to answer specific problems about the distance away people like pubs, or how many want suction to dispose of their refuse, unless these are matters which the people should raise of their own accord . . . it is the points people themselves raise, irrespective of outside suggestions, which we have tried to collect and collate.

The result of such an approach was less than definite, in as much as the range of opinions on domestic matters was very wide. Not only class, age and family, but temperament, upbringing and experience affected housing attitudes, prejudices and preferences. The importance of this survey was that it underlined the diversity of opinions on housing matters. At the same time, large numbers of people came forward with a mass of practical common sense suggestions for improving the living conditions of their homes. 'If people are to have the houses they like, these should be heard by architects and planners.' The main import of such suggestions and preferences was summarized in the Survey.

Ideal Homes
(i) The ideal house as described by interviewees varies much in size and shape. Yet it

The housing alternatives as illustrated in Liverpool.

stands out quite clearly that a large number (49%) if they could choose and other things being equal (as they never are) would live in a small house with a garden. Bungalows, though a bit less popular than small houses, nevertheless have their very considerable body of fans; slightly more than one person in ten wants to live in a bungalow. This is an amazingly high proportion and is especially notable as the proportion of existing bungalows can only be a tiny fraction of this number. People are attracted to this type of home by the absence of any stairs and the compactness of the living quarters. Many imagine that a bungalow will be more economical to run than a small house, particularly from a cleaning and heating point of view.

(ii) Flats, on the other hand, are unpopular amongst the vast mass of people, particularly those with small children . . . only 5% of the whole sample would by choice inhabit a flat . . .

(iii) Most people who want to move to a small house with a garden envisage a small modern house with plenty of labour-saving devices, self-contained and as private as possible. Yet certain people like flat life, women more than men, young rather than older people. People who do not want a garden object less to living in a flat than garden lovers; people who move about a great deal put up fewer objections to flat life than people who have lived in their houses for a great many years.

(iv) The district in which the house is situated plays its part in housing satisfaction. Half of the inhabitants of housing estates would like to go on living there, a measure of the satisfaction this type of district provides. Garden Cities came a close second. Suburbs and the country lag rather behind. Very few people would like to live in the middle of existing towns, but many people would like to live in central districts near their work and shops, if at the same time the districts were airy and provided with open spaces, gardens and trees.

Place and Situation

(i) The situation of the district, nearness to the shops, the clean healthy air, pleasant neighbours, are all factors which incline people favourably towards a particular district. Outlying districts are liked because they are open and airy, but central districts also have their advocates. These latter claim that nearness to shops and work outweighs any disadvantage the district might otherwise possess.

(ii) The situation of the house in relation to the workplace, children's schools, shops, public gardens and parks has to be taken into account before housing satisfaction can be fully assessed. In some of the more industrial areas the proximity of the house to the workplace is appreciated while in the more rural districts the openness, the trees and parks are liked.

Gardens

(i) The desire for a garden is strong in all the areas, but weakest in the places where there are in fact fewest gardens.

(ii) The majority of working class people use their gardens for the purpose of growing vegetables and flowers; many like to hang their washing out to dry. People who have not got a garden, but wish they had one, say that they too would like to grow vegetables and flowers, but many think of a garden principally as a place where they could keep chickens and sit after work and at weekends.

Bedrooms

(i) In assessing attitudes to housing, bedroom satisfaction is an important factor to be taken into account. The size and number of rooms often calls for criticism, and people with growing children especially demand at least three bedrooms. In many houses, possessing three bedrooms, the third is found to be so small as to be almost useless . . . the desire for a spare bedroom is strong in nearly all the areas surveyed.

(ii) Arrangement of bedrooms comes in for much criticism . . . people dislike bedrooms opening off the living room, bedrooms opening off each other and stairs leading up from the living room to the bedroom.

(iii) Absence of any kind of heating in bedrooms is a point of criticism. Though few people burn a fire regularly in their bedrooms, many of them like to have the opportunity for an occasional fire in case of illness or extreme cold . . . as a rule, coal fires in bedrooms are disliked; people consider them dirty and too much trouble. Electric fires, on the other hand, can be switched on for short periods and are labour saving.

Kitchens
Convenient, compact, labour-saving kitchens are in constant demand. People do not like to be cramped in their kitchen, but they do like having everything near at hand. On the other hand, kitchens must not be too small; complaints that existing ones suffer from this defect come from one person in five. One person in three suggests that houses built after the war should have large kitchens. The latter demand comes mainly from people who would like to eat as well as cook in their kitchen.

Living-rooms
People who at present have a kitchen living-room want a scullery into which to expel the gas cooker and the sink . . . people with very small sculleries sometimes want them enlarged into eating places. If people's wishes are listened to, it will in effect mean a minor revolution in working class housing. People are no longer content to live and eat in the same room; what they want today is two living rooms, one for everyday in which to eat and relax, another where visitors may be entertained and which they like to keep for best.

Bathrooms and Lavatories
Baths and bathrooms are another focal point in the present housing set-up. Whether or not a house possesses a bathroom has become a major social dividing line . . . There is a strong demand (85%) for a bathroom among the 'bathless' in this sample. Many want to see bathrooms built into existing houses. Many more feel that all houses built after the war ought to have a bathroom incorporated . . . Downstairs bathrooms are unpopular since people consider them inconvenient in case of illness. Baths built into bedrooms are disliked for the same reason. Another unpopular feature is the scullery bath, and some people had on their own initiative taken the bath away . . . Also very unpopular is the lavatory-bathroom combination . . . If the house is only to have one lavatory people either want it to be upstairs and separate from the bathroom, or downstairs, but not next to the front door, near the larder or opposite the living room.

These practical points made clear that ordinary people had very definite views on what they wanted in housing. They also demonstrated a clear awareness of a potential better future in housing. While generally willing to put up with much as far as housing conditions were concerned, they were, at the same time, capable of envisaging the sort of houses they would like: 'They are ready to help the planners and architects to build it for them'.

SOURCES

Mass-Observation Survey (1943) *Enquiry into People's Homes.*
Ministry of Health, Central Housing Advisory Committee (1944) *Design of Dwellings.*

Case Study Eighteen

The Model of Reconstruction after World War II

In 1942 the Minister of Health appointed a sub-committee of the Central Housing Advisory Committee to make recommendations as to the design, planning, layout, standards of construction and equipment of dwellings for the people throughout the country. Its report, *Design of Dwellings* (commonly known as the Dudley Report after the Chairman of the Committee, Lord Dudley), was published in 1944. Evidence was submitted to the Committee from a wide variety of sources, including those most intimately concerned, tenants and prospective tenants (see the 'People's Model' in Case Study 17).

In assessing this evidence the Committee took as its starting point the Tudor Walters Report after the First World War:

> The country has had 25 years of experience in the actual building of small houses on an unprecedented scale and is now on the threshold of a further immense housing programme. Therefore it is both timely and necessary that the subject should again be examined.

The Committee noted the changes of outlook and habit during the period which had affected the design and equipment of the houses themselves. It also placed in perspective the local-authority housing built between the wars, identifying the principal defects in accommodation:

(i) There was a lack of variety in the type of dwelling provided.

(ii) The living accommodation was too cramped and sometimes ill-adapted to the present ways of living.

(iii) Equipment and storage space was deficient in the light of advances in domestic practice.

(iv) The outbuildings were inadequate, shoddy and badly placed.

In responding to its brief the Committee ranged widely over the question of the design of dwellings, but it concentrated on these four concerns. At the same time, though the Report encompassed flats and 'specialist accommodation' in urban centres, its prime focus was the local authority suburban estate, and its general recommendations reflected the assumptions underlying such an emphasis.

Types of Dwelling

For the present we recommend that local authorities should continue in general to concentrate on the provision of the three-bedroomed house interspersed with a proportion of other types. But the distribution of the size of families, also of the types of existing

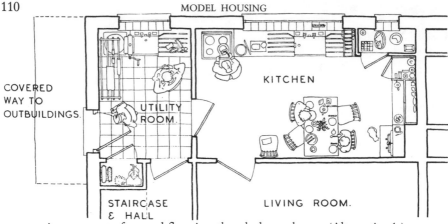

COVERED
WAY TO
OUTBUILDINGS.

UTILITY
ROOM.

KITCHEN

STAIRCASE
& HALL

LIVING ROOM.

Arrangement of ground floor in a three-bedroom house. (Alternative 1.)

dwellings, will vary considerably from place to place. There are areas where there is already a reasonably adequate supply of three-bedroomed houses. Before preparing their programmes, the local authorities should have regard to the prevailing type of house now existing in their area and the extent to which the needs of particular sizes of household remain to be met, they should be allowed considerable latitude to determine the types of dwelling necessary to meet local needs.

. . . While flats are open to many objections for families with children, they are less objectionable for other persons. There is need, therefore, for a mixed development of family houses mingled with blocks of flats for smaller households . . .

The Standard of Floor Space
. . . the municipal house of the future should provide two good rooms on the ground floor, so that meals need not interfere with other activities. We suggest that meals be taken either in a kitchen designed for the purpose, or in a dining recess off the living-room. The kitchen which is to be used for meals must be a pleasant liveable room, large enough for the table and all the kitchen fittings and equipment, and easy to keep clean and tidy. Laundry and dirty household work should not be done in a kitchen of this type but in a small separate compartment which we propose to call the 'utility room'.

Two ways were suggested of dividing up the ground floor of a modern family house, assuming that the cooking would be done by gas or electricity.

Alternative one:
Living-room 160 ft².
Kitchen, with space for meals 110 ft².
Utility room for laundry, etc. 35 ft².

Alternative two:
Living-room with recess for meals 210 ft².
Kitchen for cooking and laundry 100 ft².

These apportionments of the ground floor provide what has been the long-felt want of

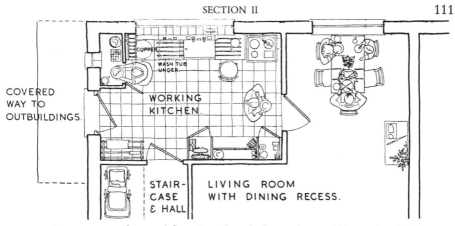

Arrangement of ground floor in a three-bedroom house. (Alternative 2.)

the average family, namely, a clean cheerful room where meals can be taken with the maximum of convenience to the housewife who does the cooking, but which is kept free from the dirty work of washing clothes, and another more private room for other activities. We think the expression 'parlour' carries an implication which is old fashioned and obsolete. Therefore we do not employ it. But we do not think it matters what these rooms are called provided that they are used to the best advantage . . .

The size of bedrooms had remained fairly constant since the Tudor Walters Report (150 ft², 100 ft², 65 ft²). In general, the committee accepted these sizes, but felt that the two smaller rooms should be slightly increased to allow for built-in furniture:

The bathroom in the inter-war house was usually on the ground floor. If, as we recommend, the living space on the ground floor is enlarged, the bathroom cannot remain there without producing a larger area on the ground floor than is required on the first floor for the bedrooms. Therefore both the bathrooms and the water closet should be upstairs. This arrangement, as our evidence has made abundantly clear, will also be far more convenient to the occupier, particularly in case of illness.

In the inter-war house the bathroom was usually combined with the water-closet. This arrangement takes up less space and is accordingly less costly. But there was much evidence that, especially in the case of large families, a combined arrangement is inconvenient. In our view it is permissible in dwellings with two bedrooms or less, but we recommend a separate water closet for dwellings with three-bedrooms.

Summarizing its views on the standard of floor space to be provided in the post war house, the committee stated:

. . . that the minimum over-all floor area that is necessary to give effect to the foregoing recommendations is 900 sq. feet, subject to slight variations according to aspect and siting. We are convinced, however, that no substantial reductions can be made in this figure if the majority of the defects in the inter-war house are to remedied. War time experience has indicated a close connection between over-crowding and morale. The nervous strain of living in too cramped quarters is an enemy of healthy family life and cannot be ignored. Rooms must be large enough both for the furniture they are to contain (which is so often of a massive nature) and for the people who are to use them. Moreover the reduction in space below a certain limit greatly increases the work of running the house and keeping it clean.

Equipment and fittings
The equipment normally provided in the inter-war dwelling consisted of a bath in the bathroom, a water closet, a sink, one draining board, a copper in the scullery, a coal range in the living-room and latterly a cooker in the scullery (where services were available), a dresser either in the living-room or scullery, built-in ventilated larder and about 20 sq. feet of shelving. Some local authorities added a wash-basin in the bathroom. Hot water was sometimes provided by a circulating system from the back boiler of the range, but more often the only hot water supply was from the copper to the bath by means of gravitation feed or a pump.

Extensive as this equipment appeared, the Committee felt it was deficient in the light of recent advances in domestic practice, and that there was need for further research and experiment on particular aspects of domestic economy:

There is an obvious need for more efficient methods of heating and maintaining a more even temperature within the dwelling.
    There is need for a heating appliance which will heat several rooms from one source. Further research is necessary into methods of economical central heating both in houses and flats . . .
    There is great need for more efficient labour-saving coal burning grates and stoves which will give more complete combustion of fuel and reduce atmospheric pollution.
    The existing types of cooker, whether for coal, gas or electricity, are all capable of improvement particularly from the point of view of conserving heat and reducing consumption of fuel.
    There is need for improvements to windows which will reduce loss of heat.
    The great advantages of new finishing materials which can be used to make attractive and easily cleaned floors, walls, window-sills, draining boards and other fittings have not yet been fully absorbed into normal building practice.

In the light of these concerns, the Committee felt that the standards of fittings and equipment in the post-war house should be based on the following principles:

(i) Where public services are connected to the dwelling there should be sufficient points to enable the tenant to make full use of labour-saving appliances.
(ii) Appliances should be selected for maximum efficiency and minimal consumption of fuel. We suggest that all appliances consuming fuel or power should be fully tested for standards of performance to be established.

The model for the post-war house thus incorporated a general raising of the level of services and equipment. This was particularly evident in the kitchen, with its fitted

Examples of different layout possibilities.

cupboards, sink, draining-boards and worksurfaces, and in the bathroom, with the availability of constant hot water, lagged plumbing and more efficient sanitary fittings. More connections for light and power made the use of electricity and gas a normal expectation.

Outbuildings and Gardens

A large number of the houses built between the wars had no outbuildings at all. Fuel was commonly stored in the body of the house with resulting dust and dirt. Nor was there any place for keeping bicycles, tools, garden produce or the numerable other things which are commonly kept in a shed . . . In other areas it was the practice for the tenants to provide their own sheds usually with most unsightly results.

In our opinion adequate outbuildings are essential to the reasonable comfort and convenience of the family. Their provision encourages many of those activities which it is the object of the new educational programme to bring about, e.g. individual hobbies, odd jobs, and active rather than passive forms of recreation. Most of these things need a shed and we accordingly recommend that appropriate outbuildings should be provided for every council house.

The size of gardens must vary according to the siting of cottages, the custom of the locality and the nature of the soil. In general the aim should be to provide as large a plot as is likely to be cultivated. A garden attached to the cottage is generally very much more popular with tenants than an allotment some way off, and is much easier for the tenant and his family to cultivate at odd moments.

In its concentration on the standards of accommodation, the fixtures and fittings and the surroundings of the dwelling, the Dudley Committee developed the best of pre-war practices, and at the same time established the new standards which were a considerable advance on Tudor Walters. However, in its concept of the housing type put forward as the model for post-war reconstruction, it was still very traditional. Though more attention was given to the needs of different groups, such as old-age pensioners and single persons, the emphasis was still on the family house, in its sub-urban surroundings, that had been the central characteristic of the model house throughout the twentieth century.

SOURCES

Ministry of Housing, Housing Advisory Committee (1944) *Design of Dwellings.*

The Prefabricated House, 1946

Though the prefabricated house of the 1940s was an emergency response to the urgent housing needs thrown up by the Second World War, it nevertheless required planning and designing from first principles. In attempting to satisfy the expectations of the housing market within tight financial constraints, prefabricated housing had to reconcile the various, and often conflicting, considerations and interests of builders and tenants. In the process, the 'prefab' became a model of what could be achieved in respect of standards of space and of equipment.

There had, of course, been experiments in the erection of buildings by different forms of prefabrication throughout the nineteenth and twentieth centuries. Cast-iron structures had been demonstrated at the Great Exhibition. The 'steel house' had been promoted after the First World War as a contribution to the twin problems of unemployment and housing shortage. There had, however, been general resistance on the part of the building industry to the introduction of new methods, new materials and new ideas. The impetus for prefabrication after the Second World War came from the examples and experience of America, where nearly eight million people had been housed in new communities, both during the New Deal and during the war years.

Reviewing this considerable technical feat in 1946, Hugh Casson rightly saw it as being of great significance for this country, in that it proved that comfortable houses could be produced quickly and in large numbers, even when both labour and money were in short supply. Co-ordinated by a National Housing Agency, which set standards of space, construction, finish and equipment, the American Housing Programme had set out to rationalize the methods and techniques of building. To achieve the speed, economy and efficiency required, the four basic principles of mass production were applied to house building:

(i) The fullest possible use of standard types and sizes in building components.
(ii) Large-scale advance ordering and bulk purchase of raw materials.
(iii) The increased use of heavy mechanical plant and powered tools served by mobile generating units.
(iv) The training of erection crews in single, quickly repetitive operations.

The experience of the structural techniques involved through this programme influenced British designers facing the insatiable post-war demand for houses of whatever type and construction. Schemes were brought forward for houses to be built by site-prefabrication, factory-prefabrication and site-assembly, and complete prefabrication and assembly at the factory. The benefits arose, on the one hand from

115

Examples of British prefabricated emergency factory-made houses.

the speed of erection and the freeing of the process from the mercies of the weather, and on the other hand from the extent to which standardization could be achieved.

It was recognized that there were two ways of applying any standard system to the design and construction of prefabricated houses. The first was to design a house of a certain type and then to mass produce it without variation. This approach limited the flexibility with which such a design could be treated. The second way was to use standard units for building. The provision of standard fitments on a national scale would effect huge savings, it was argued, while the use of standard units in the design of houses would mean that these could be re-arranged into different sizes, shapes, plans and appearance to allow for the greatest variety and flexibility. In practice, a number of types were marketed, with exterior materials as diverse as steel and resin-bonded ply-wood, and structures varying from steel frames to concrete panels. Nearly all had cavity partition walls, commonly made of plaster-board. Sanitary fitments were grouped centrally near to plumbing ducts provided with access panels for maintenance and inspection. Electrical conduits in pre-cut lengths were laid in wall and floor cavities, or behind hollow skirtings.

A typical example of the type of prefabricated house developed was that designed by F.R.S. Yorke for the Braithwaite Company of London. This was a unit-frame construction in which the frame was prefabricated, but the rest of the house, including the cladding, was put together on site. This allowed the advantages of dry assembly and standardization to be combined with a considerable amount of flexibility in the finish of the house. As the plans (page 118) show, prefabrication is in the end only a technique. It is not a type of house. However, in Yorke's approach and the emphasis on standardization there was a fundamental concern for the quality of materials used, the standards of space and equipment, and the internal arrangement of the house to allow for ease of running.

In the first place, the quantities of materials used had to be controlled if useful life was to be one of the performance-factors to be incorporated in the design formula. To this end, the value of new materials, such as plastics and resin-bonded ply-wood was examined and their application demonstrated for plumbing, floors and roofs, heat-insulation, and as surface laminates. The prefabricated house's requirement for standard-quality units encouraged the application of materials which could be modified to meet particular design requirements. Their application was extended not just by the particular demands which prefabricated houses generated in the post-war years, but also as a result of contemporary expectations. The improvements in standards of space, as recommended by the Dudley Committee, were maintained. The advantage of the prefabricated model was that, as a flexible modular design, it could be altered, added to or reduced, when required. For the first time the model was not static. The space available and its disposition could be modified to meet the particular needs of the tenant, and this was important with an increasingly mobile population.

This advance was matched by an even more emphatic improvement in the case of the provision of equipment. In the absence of encouragement, local authorities before the war tended to equip their council houses to the lowest standards consistent with 'sanitary decorum'. After the war, prefabricated houses set the pace by incorporating integrated water-heating systems, together with refrigerators, and adequate storage space, both in the kitchen and elsewhere in the house. Admittedly, in the first years of the re-housing programme, the provision of house carcasses outstripped the

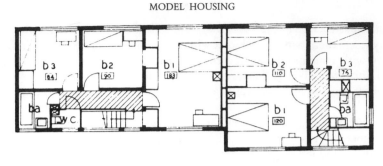

House 1   House 2

149. FIRST FLOOR

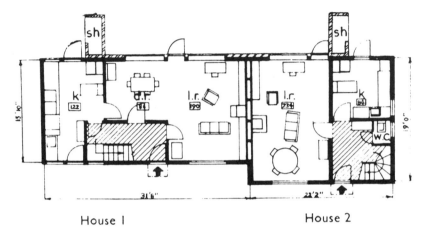

House 1   House 2

150. GROUND FLOOR

KEY :

b1, b2, b3	bedrooms
ba	bathroom
lr . . .	living-room
dr	dining-room
k	kitchen
sh	shed

Hall and landing hatched.

AREAS :

House 1   960 sq. ft.
House 2   810 sq. ft.
Room areas in sq. ft. as marked on plans.

The Braithwaite house plans.

production of such equipment, but its inclusion in the standard fittings of the house was allowed for in the design process.

What could be achieved in respect of standards of space and equipment was also achieved in respect of ease of running. This again was largely a matter of design, and great thought was put into the details of design in the prefabricated house, from

The kitchen of a British 'prefab'.

windows which could be cleaned from inside the room, to covered skirtings to eliminate dust traps. When it came to surfaces, the resources of modern technology did much to eliminate time-absorbing finishes and to achieve a high degree of labour-saving. Mass-produced materials could bring these within the reach of every home and make the life of the housewife far less arduous. 'It is possible, therefore, to look at the future from an entirely new aspect. Instead of a miscellaneous collection of appliances, we now have one comprehensive household service . . .'

The prefabricated house, by isolating and identifying the design problem, encouraged and enabled the fullest and most imaginative use of technical resources to achieve such a comprehensive solution.

SOURCES

Anthony, H. (1945) *Houses: Permanence and Prefabrication.* London: Pleiades Books.

Casson, H. (1946) *Homes by the Million.* Harmondsworth: Penguin.

Madge, J. (1946) *Tomorrow's Houses.* London: Pilot Press.

Ministry of Works (1944) *Housing Equipment.*

The Festival of Britain, 1951: Live Architecture

The ostensible purpose of the Festival of Britain was to commemorate the centenary of the Great Exhibition; in practice it was designed to demonstrate the country's recovery from war. It was the means by which the post-war government set out to present to the people the ideals and goals of the 'new society'. The Festival of Britain offered, in the words of Roy Strong:

> . . . an enchanted glass in which somehow the organisers shorn of the magic of Empire, attempted to reconstitute a future based on a new secular mythology. . . . it made tangible to the masses the Utopia of the Welfare State, the salvation of society seen in terms of universal material provision, education and nationalisation. It was the world of the Education Act, the Town & Country Planning Act, the National Insurance Act, the New Towns and the National Health Service, conjured into a momentary millenary vision.

This vision and enterprise has to be placed against the background of a country, and particularly a capital city, that had suffered much devastation and was in a depressing state of dejection and deterioration. There was a sense of urgency to do something about these new problems and also those that had proved insoluble between the wars. In the light of new demands, as well as new developments, there was a feeling of enterprise in the building and construction trade. It was therefore decided that, along with the main Festival Exhibition, there should be an exhibition of building which would be designed to be of value and interest, not only to the professional, but also to the general public, 'who had only the vaguest ideas of what the "New Britain" would actually be like'.

The 'Live Architecture Exhibition,' which intended to show the British achievement in architecture, town planning and building research, was located on the East India Dock Road and represented one of the new neighbourhoods proposed in the plan for bomb-damaged Poplar. The estate was called 'Lansbury' after the veteran Labour politician from the area. The scheme was the responsibility of the L.C.C. and is summarized in its press handout:

> The buildings of varying heights will be grouped around closes and spaces of different sizes, each with its individual character. In some cases there will be children's playgrounds in the centre of blocks, completely protected from traffic. The layout is in fact a series of neighbourly groups linked together by open spaces. While this type of layout

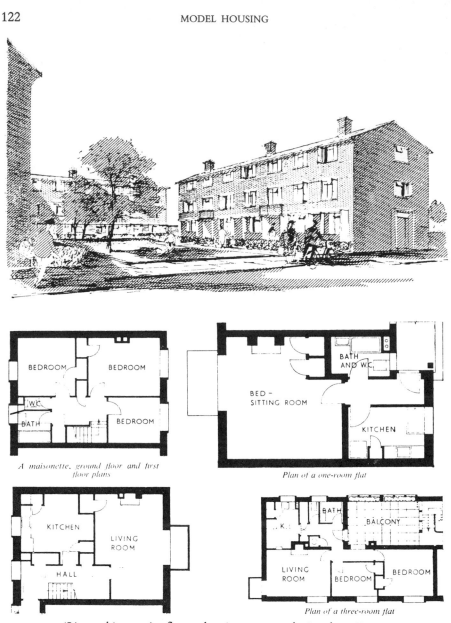

A maisonette, ground floor and first
floor plans

Plan of a one-room flat

Plan of a three-room flat

'Live architecture' – flats and maisonettes on the Lansbury Estate.

is new to the East End of London and the contrast between new and old forms of
development is likely to prove striking, the architectural treatment of most of the
buildings will include the use of London stock bricks and purple grey slates which are
traditional building materials for this part of Poplar.

The intention was to combine innovation with tradition, and the Exhibition

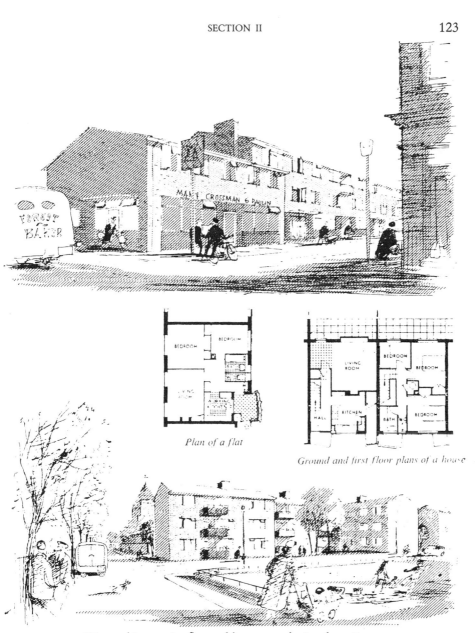

Plan of a flat

Ground and first floor plans of a house

'Live architecture' – flats and houses on the Lansbury Estate.

provided a model of the different kinds of development planned. The emphasis was not just on building techniques and styles, but also on the planned relationship of buildings and space. Lansbury was also conceived in relation to the County of London Plan of 1943, which placed the question of housing and open spaces in the broader context of residential distribution and mobility. The plan sought to revive the sense of communities and neighbourhood units within the total development and dispersal of the city.

The Live Architecture Exhibition was a cross-section of a neighbourhood, designed to demonstrate the model of proper planning of space and buildings. The 30-acre site contained not only completed buildings but also some in the course of erection in order to demonstrate modern methods of construction. These was also a Town Planning Pavilion and a Building Research Pavilion, in which there were diagrams and models explaining the principles to be followed in providing for a new community.

Though several architects were involved in designing the houses at Lansbury, there was close overall control of the development to ensure coherence of design and layout. Standards were laid down with regard to the desired proportions of housing units, the daylight requirements, access arrangements and the apportionment of buildings and open spaces. This approach gave the scheme significance as one of the first occasions when so many buildings were designed simultaneously by many architects working in unison under the guidance of a team of planners.

The result was housing in terraces and low blocks of flats forming pleasant spaces. The shopping centre and market square was a three-storey development of maisonettes over shops; there were two public houses and a market hall. All this was located in a pedestrian precinct – the first to be built in London. Existing schools were incorporated in the plan and two new churches provided. The site was divided into four residential sections, in which there was living accommodation for about 1500 people in 400 or more dwellings, which comprised flats, houses and maisonettes. The blocks of flats had three or six storeys, each flat with from one to four rooms with kitchen, bathroom and wc in addition. The separate houses had two, and in some cases three floors with similar or greater accommodation and small private gardens. The maisonettes, which were two-storey dwellings, were in three or four-storey blocks over shops with private gardens or small terraces.

The construction of the houses and flats was generally traditional, with load-bearing walls of brick and roofs of slate. A variety of floor constructions was used which demonstrated not only normal wooden boards and joists and in the flats fire-resistant concrete constructions, but also special proprietary types. Floor surfaces were finished in various plastic compositions, and in the flats all the plumbing was internal and contained in ducts within the structure. The standard of provision within the housing accommodation is reflected in this description of the maisonettes on the North Site:

> All maisonettes have private gardens at the front and rear. The living room and dining space on the ground floor have been planned as a through room partially divided by the chimney breast. Access to the rear garden is from the dining space, leaving the maximum wall area for fittings and equipment in the kitchen. On the first floor the maisonettes have either three or four bedrooms with built-in cupboards, a bathroom and wc.

The most important feature of the scheme was the diversity of accommodation

Gremlin Grange.

presented, both in terms of type and size. This included special provision for old people. There was a 'home' equipped for old people unable to manage for themselves. Within some of the blocks of flats provision was also made for old people who were still able to manage for themselves; each unit had a bed-sitting room, kitchen, combined bathroom and wc. Gardens were specially laid out for older people, with sheltered seats.

Perhaps the most novel feature of this model was that, while the buildings themselves were conventional and unadventurous, they were related to an exhibition which showed how good and economical building depended on scientific methods developed from well-directed research, and explained the principles of good planning and sound building. The idea was that practice should follow precept, and to illustrate the dangers of not doing so there was the ultimate in model houses – the anti-model. This was called 'Gremlin Grange' and was a full-sized demonstration of how things might go wrong when scientific principles in building were ignored – structural cracks in walls, leaning walls and chimneys, rising damp, peeling plaster, smokey fireplaces and bad lighting. This was intended as an object lesson in how not to build a house.

In contrast, Lansbury had the air of 'something brave, something new, something exciting . . . it looked gay, exciting, colourful'. Of this Frederick Gibberd recalls:

As an environment it was at that time a revelation. Bright, cheerful and human in scale, it formed an exciting contrast with its drab and derelict setting. In planning terms it showed the advantages of comprehensive development, how different kinds of building can be arranged to form pleasant urban spaces . . . Even though it has been cruelly neglected, the development still has an air of quiet distinction and, though it may be dated architecturally, it is a place with its own character: an intimate, friendly and human character, which planners and architects are now seeking to revive.

SOURCES

Banham, M. & Hillier, B. (eds.) (1976) *A Tonic to the Nation*. London: Thames and Hudson.

Dunnett, H. McG. (ed.) (1951) *Guide to the Exhibition of Architecture, Town Planning and Building Research (Poplar)*. London: Festival of Britain.

The Impact
of the Model House

The Impact
of the Model House

By examining the model house, and its development over time, it is possible to establish what housing reformers, commentators and practitioners believed should constitute a proper home for the working man and his family. Such houses demonstrate the changing attitudes and approaches to design, and show how contemporary stylistic ideas and innovations were translated into a range of housing types. The model did not, however, simply respond to current concepts and take up and incorporate stylistic features and fashions; it did itself generate a sense of what was expected and required.

This characteristic was clear from the outset in the earliest articulation of the model labourer's cottage. By 1850, as a result of the involvement and interest of aristocratic landowners and agricultural reform societies, and more particularly as a result of the collection and publication of model plans in pattern books and periodicals, there existed a clear expectation of what the model village, and within it the model labourer's cottage, should look like.

The concept had changed from the excesses of the Picturesque pattern books, with their emphasis on what Uvedale Price had referred to as 'the characteristic beauties of a village . . . intricacy, variety and play of outline'.[1] Nevertheless, the concern was still to achieve an idealized cottage style with some roots in tradition. The emphasis was on an overlay of decoration and detail, deriving from a debased sense of the vernacular and an imperfect understanding of the Gothic style.

By the middle of the nineteenth century, however, it was beginning to be recognized that visual qualities alone were not enough to ensure model dwellings. John Claudius Loudon, especially, had done much, in his various writings, to draw attention to the designs of cottages made by the devotees of the Picturesque, which he recognized might be of beauty and interest but which were nonetheless quite impracticable. At the same time he had, through various editions of his Encyclopaedia, brought to the attention of landowners and architects the kind of design he advocated for comfortable practical dwellings whose layout and appearance clearly reflected their purpose.

Architecturally, it was agreed that the principal expense should be bestowed on the porches, windows, and chimneys; style was to be both consistent and relatively simple, and appropriate to the occupation of the inhabitants; ornament, while restrained, should not be lacking. Cottages were to be well provided in terms of both their construction and facilities: the walls were to be strong and solid, assuring dryness and warmth, compared with traditional labourers' dwellings; the designs to allow for the greatest amount of accommodation with the available floor space; the cottages not to be placed directly onto the road, but set back to give an informal appearance and to allow an appropriate alignment for the sun; the minimum of three bedrooms to allow for separation in the sleeping arrangements of the boys and girls of the family; the accommodation to include a work-room and a living-room, but no un(der)-used parlour; the gardens to be at least a rood (a quarter acre), enabling cottagers not only to produce vegetables and potatoes, but also to keep a pig and poultry.

The gardens were recognized as an important adjunct to the model cottage for, as Loudon argued, they allowed for 'recreation that was not idleness, but rather a change in kind and degree of labour and occupation'. Gardens, it was hoped, would improve the standard of living of the rural labourer and strengthen those bonds which linked him to the social fabric of the country. At the same time, cottages had to be planned to encourage that privacy and separation of families which the middle classes saw as an essential first step to social responsibility and respectability. The collection together of dwellings in villages was not without its disadvantages, and the provisions of the 'model village', it was argued, would overcome some of these. Cottages were seen as very much part of the total development of church, school and alms-houses; in this context it was envisaged that the provision of a comfortable home would encourage a sense of property amongst the tenancy and thereby strengthen their 'social affections and local attachments' and render them 'in every way . . . better members of society'.[2]

These sentiments were very much reflected in the response of some nineteenth-century industrialists to the question of improved housing for their workforces and the development of model industrial communities. As has been shown in the case of Akroyden, there was there an explicit desire to represent both managerial interests and a social concern for the inhabitants in the design and appearance of the houses. However the extent of such involvement was limited, and care must be taken not to generalize from one model or to assume philanthropic motives where none existed. Detailed investigation of industrial housing makes clear that involvement was only rarely related either to a philanthropic ideal or to a desire to create a more satisfactory environment. In the majority of cases, those industrialists who built houses did so for reasons either of managerial necessity or as a means of capital investment.

In the first stages of industrialization, the practicalities of managerial necessity had compelled industrialists to participate in the provision of houses for their workforces. Such housing schemes were part of a whole pattern of settlements which Marshall has described as 'coming into being through one major decision or a comparatively limited succession of major decisions'.[3] As a result of this process, settlement occurred on sites selected because various economic factors were there present in combination. If this meant a site where there was no workforce near at hand, then the management must perforce be responsible for housing the necessary immigrant population, and in many cases, where there was no public organization, responsible for basic services.

By the middle of the nineteenth century, however, housing provision was no longer a primary concern of industrialists catering for a large immigrant workforce. By then the industrial areas of the North and Midlands were well developed, and it was rare for a works or mill to be situated beyond walking distance from an established community. This tendency was extended over the middle years of the century, as changing power requirements occasioned the increasing conglomeration of industry and furthered the process of urbanization. As a result, by the middle years of the nineteenth century, few industrialists felt obliged to provide houses for their workers for reasons of managerial necessity; and as in most cases the building was not of an appreciably higher standard then other working class housing in the district, it does not appear that there was any great concern with the improvement of standards. The majority of industrialists probably regarded housing less as a social obligation than as a further channel of capital at times of expansion.

This was as true of industrialists operating on relatively isolated sites as it was of those whose works were situated in expanding urban communities. Moreover, it was as true of the small manufacturer as it was of the large firm, The former, like the hundreds of small-scale building speculators who financed the working class housing of every nineteenth-century town, gradually developed the house property under their control as their business and capital expanded.

Clearly, by this time the use of houses by industrialists as a means of discipline and control over their workers was less necessary, and therefore less important, than it had been in the first stages of the Industrial Revolution. The impact of industrial housing on the creation of a model workforce has probably been overrated as a result of the attention it received from the critics of the factory system in the 1830s and 1840s. Peter Gaskell, writing of Manchester, saw this as the main reason which induced manufacturers to build houses.[4] In practice, by the middle years of the nineteenth century, few industrialists appear to have limited the tenancy of such houses as they built to their own workers.

Nevertheless, within even the best regulated establishments the fact that housing could be made a means of managerial control was a matter of criticism. For instance, the Chartist pamphleteer, McDouall, claimed that at Hyde, where Thomas Ashton provided his workers with four-roomed stone built cottages, the operatives' freedom of action was curtailed because of the deduction from their wages of the employer's dues as landlord for the house, coal and water, along with 2d. a week towards a Sunday School and the drawbacks of fines.[5] As late as 1871, there was similar criticism of Hugh Mason's housing activities in Ashton-under-Lyne. Workers complained that they could only get a job in his mills if they accepted the house allocated to them. As a result, it was claimed that Mason could charge four shillings per week rent for houses which elsewhere in the town would only raise three shillings.

Whatever the motives behind managerial involvement in housing, there seems little doubt that such provision was, in general, profitable investment even for those firms which chose to rise above the minimum of contemporary standards. All housing ventures, including those with an overtly philanthropic character, were expected to provide an adequate financial return. Admittedly, Salt was willing to let cottages at Saltaire, which had cost from £120 to £200 each to build, for rents varying from 2s. 4d. to 7s. 6d. per week. The return on his capital investment of approximately 4 per cent was thus less than the 5–6 per cent normally expected from

commercial investments and would have been acceptable to few other manufacturers. Indeed, Edward Akroyd's model village at Copley near Halifax averaged a
return of only about 4½ per cent on the outlay, and of this Akroyd commented:

> In a financial respect the Copley experiment is not very successful; and it may be
> doubted whether any landlord building good cottages for tenantry, or a mill owner for
> his work people, can obtain a rent which would pay the ordinary rate of interest for
> cottage property.[6]

It was the low financial reward from this undertaking that induced Akroyd to seek
other means of housing improvement, as has been seen at Akroyden. However,
Akroyd's pessimism does, on the whole, seem less than justified. A manufacturer did
not have to rely on insanitary slum property for a more than adequate return on his
property. By the middle years of the century such property could be expected to
provide a financial return of between 10 and 12 per cent, while the 'improved
housing' of industrialists brought an estimated gross return of between 7 and 9 per
cent.

For example, in 1836 W. & M. Christy erected thirty-five cottages adjoining their
Fairfield Mills at Droylsden, which had been opened the preceding year. These were
well-built parlour cottages with individual yards and privies, and costing between
£100 and £120 each. During the following five years the firm was receiving a steady
8–9 per cent return on the property.

The Ashworths, with their famous mill villages at Egerton and Turton, always
expected an economic return from their housing, despite its high standard. William
Dodd, the factory cripple, described the Ashworth cottages:

> . . . they are good substantial stone buildings, roomy, well-drained, well-lighted,
> well-watered, and well-aired, having one door in front, and another at the back . . .[7]

The rents on these cottages were always intended to bring in a gross return of
between 7 and 10 per cent and a net return of 6 per cent and Boyson has calculated
that on average the firm received a gross return of 8.3 per cent and a net return of 5.2
per cent. In general, when the manufacturer was providing houses of a quality
basically comparable with those normally erected in the neighbourhood, he could
expect a slightly higher return than the ordinary builder, since he did not have to
make allowances for empty houses and commonly had less difficulty in rent
collection.

This financial consideration was the basic interest of most of those industrialists
who undertook housing. Thus when it is remembered that it was only a minority, in
any case, who were involved in housing of any kind, it was clearly a very small
number who were building for philanthropic reasons or whose primary interest was
the provision of better living conditions for their workers. The majority of industrialists who did build did not erect houses that were either significantly worse or
better than other houses built in their locality. It was indeed a very small number of
industrialists who made any contribution to the process of housing reform in the

nineteenth century. The benefits of better housing seem to have come very low in the estimation of the vast majority of industrialists. For even among those manufacturers who were concerned to provide other forms of social welfare there was an apparent lack of interest in housing.

The very small amount of 'improved housing' provided by industrialists meant that as such it made a limited contribution to the housing stock in the nineteenth century. However, in terms of its contribution to the developing pattern of housing-reform ideas and ideals it was important. The model improved housing of industrialists emphasized the differing approaches to housing reform. Some industrialists had an ideal of amelioration and wished to improve the standard of working class living accommodation. Within that number there were those who had an ideal of a village community and of the benefits, other than simply the quality of accommodation, that this would mean for the working people; and beyond this there were some industrialists who promoted the idea of giving architectural expression to these concepts of community building. The promotion of this endeavour, in a very few special cases, was a particular contribution of nineteenth-century industrialists to the developing theories of housing reform and planning.

Most of the so-called model houses built by industrialists did not make any radical departure from traditional forms and concepts. If they were products of the desire to ameliorate the living conditions of the workers, to that end they were built in accord with more stringent specifications, and with more extensive or better arranged accommodation. Such considerations had been the concern of those industrialists, such as the Ashworths of Bolton and Ashton of Hyde, who had sought to improve the basic quality of their workers' accommodation during the 1830s and 1840s, and whose efforts were so frequently quoted as evidence of what could be achieved by philanthropically inclined manufacturers.

At Egerton, Henry and Edmund Ashworth built cottages for between £80 and £100. In most cases these were three-or four-bedroomed houses with a living room, back-kitchen, and pantry downstairs. Each house had a separate outside lavatory in a walled and private back yard, and at New Eagley small gardens fenced with iron railings were attached. 'Nothing can be more commodious than these cottages, in which the interior appearance invites to order and cleanliness.'[8] Plans and details of the cottages were published in the Report of the Poor Law Commissioners on the Sanitary Condition of the Labouring Population of Great Britain as an example for others to follow.

Very few did follow the example, but of those industrialists who did strive to ameliorate the living conditions of their workers, most restricted their efforts to the securing of basic standards of construction and decency. For instance, when between 1860 and 1871 Hugh Mason established outside Ashton-under-Lyne his new Oxford Mills with a group of 113 associated cottages, the latter were virtually indistinguishable from any contemporary bye-law street, apart from the occasional brick and terracotta embellishment on the gables or the string-course in blue Staffordshire bricks. The fact, however, that the cottages cost around £240 each was indicative of their more substantial construction. Accommodation was also more generous, in that only twenty cottages had just two bedrooms, ninety had three each and the remainder four.

A clear expression of the motivation behind such activity is contained in a paper by S. Rollinson, the Chesterfield architect, who in 1868 designed the model cottages adjoining the Kiverton Park Colliery of the Duke of Leeds. He stated:

> It was his endeavour to erect at as small an outlay as possible houses containing the greatest amount of accommodation and comfort upon a reasonable area of space, suitable for the majority of our workers yet bearing in mind that essential – sound construction.[9]

To achieve his objective of models of utility, not ornament, he said that pictorial effects must be dispensed with as unnecessary and misplaced. He thought that the cottages should be close to the pit-head, so as to reduce unpunctuality as well as to obviate the need for workers to waste their strength by walking a great distance, and give them an opportunity for using their spare time in the garden. The allotment gardens were a central feature of the Kiverton Park scheme. The houses themselves all had six rooms – a significant increase in accommodation on the traditional miners' cottages.

The management at Kiverton Park found it to its advantage to provide such houses, coupled with higher wages, for they claimed that their class of workman was regulated to a great extent by the class of house they provided. Downstairs the houses had a small parlour and a living-room which was fitted with a slop stone with running water which drained out into an open channel. Upstairs there were three bedrooms, all properly ventilated and fitted with cupboards and pegs, intended to 'suggest habits of neatness to the occupants'. Each house had a separate yard, properly flagged and drained, and with an individual privy at the furthest point from the house. Also at Kiverton Park, every six houses were provided with a wash-house so that the house itself might be kept tidy and free of steam. The inconvenience of laundering within the confines of a small house was considered by many housing reformers and temperance workers as one of the foremost causes driving men to the warmth and comfort of the public house.

The advantages to the industrialist in the control and supervision of his workforce when it was concentrated on a rural site were readily appreciated, and indeed some manufacturers, in the third quarter of the century, made the conscious decision to move their works and their workforce out of the towns to isolated settings. The advantages of moving to a rural site were seized on by the Yorkshire housing reformer, James Hole. In support of this transition, he wrote:

> If the workers are badly housed, he [the owner] will lose much in their absence through sickness, and still more by their idleness and wastefulness, the result of their low moral feelings and want of self-respect. If they have to walk a considerable distance to their work, the mere loss of physical energy and effectiveness is considerable in the course of a year. Large factory owners have often admitted that whatever they have spent in improving the education and social condition of the work-people has been a

most profitable investment; and surely among all the positive conditions of improvement none are so powerful as a clean, comfortable and healthy dwelling.[10]

In addition to the advantages gained by having a healthy workforce, the nineteenth-century industrialists, at sites removed from the town, were also able to enjoy a degree of control over their workforce that was comparable with that of the early factory masters of the eighteenth century. Management saw the control that this gave them as a means of protecting their workers from the demoralizing features of the town. This had been the motive behind Titus Salt's transference of his mills and workforce away from the evil environment of Bradford to the new rural site on the banks of the Aire. In the following decade, the establishment of new works at Bromborough Pool was evidence of a similar concern by Prices to remove their works and workers out of the slums of Battersea. Similarly, in 1860 with the establishment of what was to be known as 'Holdsworth's Philanthropic Venture' at Reddish near Stockport, W.H. Holdsworth closed his spinning mills in the congested centre of Manchester and, by means of better houses and the provision of a school, club and church, attracted his workforce to a new site in the country. In all these cases, it was to the owners' advantage to move out to new sites where there was room for expansion on cheap land, but they were all equally conscious of the benefits inherent in such moves for their work-people and for the strengthening of the ties between the industrialist and his labour-force.

It was the realization of the advantages gained by moving away from the increasingly over-crowded urban centres into rural sites that was probably the most significant contribution of nineteenth-century industrialists to a developing pattern of housing reform and planning. Admittedly the number of such undertakings was small, but they provided practical expression of the belief that people's lives and welfare would be determined by their environment, and that the 'better life' would be secured only in a retreat from urbanity.

Out of this activity arose the desire to give architectural expression to the concept of a community, and to create a visually satisfying settlement. The most coherent statement of this idealization of the village community was to be found in Akroyden. Edward Akroyd began to formulate his ideas at Copley in the previous decade. There, though the back-to-back cottages were placed in long parallel rows, they were given facades in a consciously Gothic style, with steep roofs, mullioned windows and pointed gables. As Akroyd wrote:

A Picturesque outline was adopted in a modified old English style, approximating to the character of many old dwellings in the neighbourhood . . .[11]

Here was a claimed attachment to the architecture of the past. It involved a search after an environment which it was believed would express the concept of a community in which there were close ties between master and men, and which re-created, to some degree, a supposed feudal ideal.

Such model cottages were consciously created artefacts. They were designed to reflect a mediaeval ideal; but a clear understanding of mediaeval vernacular architecture was only slowly evolving over the middle years of the century, and these models demonstrate the still limited appreciation of the architectural profession. Likewise, none of the industrial communities which have been referred to demonstrate any advance in terms of layout and planning concepts. None varied greatly from the rigidity of parallel terraces, and few deviated from a grid-iron layout. For all its high standards and architectural embellishments, Saltaire remained bound by its pattern of right-angles. Equally rigid was the plan of Holdsworth's Philanthropic Venture at Reddish. Laid out in open country, the five parallel streets of housing, with narrow back-alleys between, run at right-angles to a spine that centred on the mill clock. All the institutional buildings were placed along the boundary street at one edge of the estate. In planning, as in architecture, the industrial settlement of the middle years of the nineteenth century did not demonstrate relatively new or less formal modes of development.

Of the minority of industrialists who undertook house-building, only a small number endeavoured to improve the standards of the dwellings, and a mere handful perceived the problem in terms of a community of houses as distinct from a customary small group of houses. If in quantitative terms nineteenth-century industrialists made a very limited contribution to the housing pattern of the century, the demonstration by a few of them of the benefits of community life when removed from the unpleasantness and pressures of the urban setting did make a significant contribution to housing-reform.

By the 1870s the model houses and initiatives of both idealists and well-intentioned industrialists had amounted to only a small number of planned estates and housing for a few thousand people. These were of limited significance compared with the extensive development of model tenements by the various housing trusts and companies and, though such schemes provided ideas and guidelines for future development, they did not present a practical solution to the Victorian housing problem. That was largely to come in the third quarter of the century from models of a very different kind, as incorporated in local bye-law controls, and from 1875 onwards in national legislation and guidelines. The nature of these controls arose from the continuing concern for health reform, developing from the work of Chadwick in the 1840s.

Over the middle years of the century both sanitarians and social reformers pressed for greater intervention in the housing market if the standards of the housing of the masses were to be raised. The concern was with basic standards, and with securing basic provision in terms of light, air and space in the layout of housing and urban areas. These fundamental principles to be observed in the planning of houses were laid down at the first meeting of the Social Science Association in 1857, when Rev. C.H. Hartshorn commented:

> A sunny aspect gives cheerfulness to the inmates more than any artificial stimulates that can be supplied. It elevates the spirit at the commencement of the day and sends forth the workman in pleasant courage to his labour, and besides this it imparts a genial warmth to his dwelling which no amount of heat can produce.[12]

The more spacious planning of houses was urged not only so as to secure the admittance of a greater degree of sunlight, but also to allow the free circulation of fresh air. The consequences of over-building were clearly spelt out by George Godwin at the Social Science Congress in 1864 when he posed the question, 'What is the influence on health of the overcrowding of dwelling houses and workshops?':

> Passing the greater part of their lives deprived of that without which there is no life, pure air, a low state of health becomes chronic: they exist, do not live. Bad air takes away the appetite, depresses the spirit, lessens the vital power and predisposes to more serious disease.[13]

The circulation of fresh air led inevitably to the practicalities of ventilation. Much discussion on the subject was involved with the problem of securing the most effective flow of air within a house, both by means of better layout and by the use of mechanical ventilating devices However, increasing attention was given to the circulation of air around the buildings and the need to deal with the overall layout of an area, rather than simply to improve the individual dwelling-house. When H.H. Collins sought to answer the question, 'What provisions are required in a general Building Act so as to secure effective sanitary arrangements?', he postulated the basic requirement that all streets should be open and that alleys and culs-de-sac should be abolished:

> It should be enacted that for every house *exclusively* there should be a back yard of a minimum depth of ten feet by the whole width of the house, and that no party fence or wall should be erected more than seven feet high. So back to backs would be swept away, through ventilation provided, because passages will be constructed through houses from back to front and windows likewise. Sun, light and air, those best and perfect prophylactic agents, which seldom penetrate the foulness and darkness of a London dwelling, would permeate throughout not only the houses but also the neighbourhood, carrying with them health to a debilitated frame, strength to the weak and doing much to solve the important problem of how best to improve the habits and and homes of the poor and middle classes.[14]

Yet though adequate ventilation and the abundant provision of light and air were recognized as the vital pre-requisites of a healthy dwelling, the incorporation of the necessary features in the layout of housing was only to be ensured by statutory enforcement. As the Medical Officer for the Mile End Old Town noted in his report of 1876:

> Water, air, light are nature's disinfectants and preventors of disease. They are abundantly provided but more meagerly and inefficiently used, and indeed practically ignored by architects, builders, owners and occupiers . . .[15]

These complaints reflected the misgivings expressed by Dr. Lethaby, the Medical Officer for the City of London, as early as 1862. He observed that, though much attention had been given to the subject of sanitary improvement and the dangers inherent in the dense overcrowding of the population in ill-ventilated courts and alleys, efforts at alleviation had been almost nullified by 'the passive resistance of landlords and by the sullen indifference of the poor'. The need for action was imperative:

> Until, indeed, the latter can be made to feel the advantage of an improved social condition, and can be taught that human beings ought not to breed together like brute beasts, it will be hardly possible to lessen the death rate of our large cities, or to keep down the unwholesome influences which are ever fostering endemic disease. This kind of duty is fast becoming an obligation of society for it is perceived that the evils of such ignorance are not confined to the poor alone. They spread among the rich and largely affect the interests of all.[16]

Clearly, legislative enactments would be essential to enforce the necessary sanitary and spatial reforms. In 1864 George Godwin, in his pamphlet *Another Blow for Life*, pleaded for legal interference and the application of building Acts to ensure better standards of light, air and ventilation, and for adequate inspection in order to prevent overcrowding. The implementation of satisfactory standards, it was increasingly realized, would depend on local authorities having powers to guard against the overcrowding of a site and the placing of buildings so as to obscure the proper supply of light and air from others. In short, powers to govern the spatial standards of housing layout were needed.

These developed, in response to this public health debate, in both the metropolis and most large provincial towns during the 1860s. Many of the bye-laws, however, had gaps within them and lacked legislative precision. It was to bring administrative rationalization to this situation that the Public Health Act of 1875 was passed. Its importance lay not only in its comprehensiveness, but also in its clear format and definition of the powers of local authorities over building controls. The way in which these should be interpreted was set out in the Model Bye-Laws produced by the Local Government Board in 1877, which have been examined in Case Study 7. Here the model is used to determine the minimum standards of building and to establish the acceptable norm for speculative housing.

As a result of the acceptance of these spatial standards, overcrowding of buildings was recognized as a major threat, not just to the physical well-being of the populace, but also to their moral welfare. James Morrison, the Chairman of the Committee of Management of the Glasgow Improvement Trusts, summed up the dangers to the inhabitants of overcrowded areas:

> As well might we expect a plant to flourish when deprived of the refreshing light and dews of heaven, as that virtuous life could exist in such a region, living in a tainted atmosphere without either the decencies or conveniences of life, surrounded by a mass of poverty and dirt, without contact with anything in the locality to elevate or stimulate to improvement; without, as has been well expressed, anything to remind one either of God or nature, it would be strange indeed if these districts were not to show, as they do, all the characteristics of pauperism, intemperance and crime.[17]

High density was clearly established as a factor in itself which prevented the experience of the good life. Sanitarians feared the direct correlation between high density and the prevalence of disease with its ensuing high death rate. As it was not determined whether this relationship held true in the high densities of the new tenement-blocks, many housing-reformers and sanitarians assumed that it was so. Despite much conflicting evidence, they included in their arguments all areas of high density regardless of the housing-pattern employed. There were some, however, who considered block-dwellings, of whatever quality, to have a greater threat to health than densely-packed traditional dwellings. As a result, in London particularly, newer tenement schemes were considered, along with older areas of overcrowding, as productive of bad conditions and indicative of the need for low-density, low-rise housing.

High density thus aroused strong and often unwarranted prejudices, and came to be associated with a particular kind of housing which was usually on a scale which was large and inhuman. Reforming concern over the sanitary aspects of conventional tenement buildings combined with other criticisms of model dwellings to produce a positive movement in favour of an alternative answer to the problem of housing the working class population in large cities. The flat-dwellings were unpopular among those for whom they were intended. Overtones of charity and the connotations of barrack-building combined with the working classes' natural antipathy to organization and regulation. Lethaby reported in 1862:

> Even model lodging houses are by no means universally popular. They are always wholesome and convenient, but they involve restraints to which the poor are unwilling to submit. Admission is by a kind of favour and occupation by sufferance. Regulations are imposed as necessary indeed and unobjectionable in themselves, but still obnoxious in the sight of the applicants. They want to be independent and rather than yield that goal they will put up with any amount of dirt and discomfort.[18]

The form of building had, however, always been justified on grounds of economic necessity in areas of high land values. The opposition was thus greatly strengthened when it could be demonstrated that even by building high in central areas the housing companies had not been able to produce dwellings within the reach of the labouring population. In 1875 *The Architect* summed up these misgivings in a sharp rejoinder to Henry Darbishire's exposition to the Architectural Institute of the virtues of block building:

> Not only are these elephantine asylums unsightly to the eye, out of accord with one's ideas of the fitness of things and abhorrent to a sense of independence in probably 99 per cent of the working people of this city, but it is now officially intimated that they involve an utter sacrifice from first and last of everything like even the simplest commercial principles and investment and return. When let out at the by no means inconsiderable rents of from £6. 10s. for one little room to £16. 5s. for four little rooms per annum, it seems they pay 5 per cent – some authorities say only 4 per cent – upon the builder's bill; leaving out of account altogether the freehold site, the

drainage and sewerage, the formation of ground surface, the fencing and other sundries, as if they cost nothing at all instead of perhaps almost twice as much in some cases as the buildings themselves.[19]

The journal considered that it was no solution to the problem if the working classes could only be decently housed by means of the contributions of philanthropists. It was felt that the architectural profession should endeavour to evolve a housing pattern which would meet the needs and means of the class for whom it was intended. It was, of course, part of the problem that during the 1860s architects had as a profession neglected the problem of working class housing. The design of large tenement blocks was monotonous, and the planning of the site often paid little attention to the needs of aspect or ventilation, but simply sought to crowd as many tenants as possible onto a small unit of land. Economic pressures prevented housing companies from acknowledging environmental considerations, and the uniform design largely employed for such tenements did nothing to improve the architectural quality of these buildings, whose drab and forbidding appearance contributed to their unpopularity:

> Bearing in mind the weaknesses of the architectural initiative and the low level of creative inspiration, it is not surprising that the buildings are direct – at times downright crude – expressions of their function, without the slightest attempt to create a visual amenity which would make them pleasing to live in or a worthy addition to our towns.[20]

The street facades and general external appearance of these model dwellings were widely condemned by contemporaries. As a result, in this context the term 'model' came to have the same connotation as when used in relation to workhouses and prisons, and reflected an attitude to the poor that was at once repressive and reforming. The promoters of these model tenements hoped that their dwellings would raise the standards of working class living while reinforcing their social status. The early blocks were grim and gaunt, with plain repetitive facades, which were only relieved in those built after 1860 by Peabody and Waterlow through the addition of irrelevant decorative features. But, on the whole, decoration had to be limited so that dwellings could be made to pay. As a result, Tarn has concluded that: 'Design, as a creative skill, played no part in the considerations of nearly all the societies and companies that worked before 1880.'[21]

This is ironic, for the promoters of such model dwellings set out to raise the moral standards and behaviour of the tenants through the quality and appearance of the buildings. It was also unfortunate in that the emphasis in contemporary criticism on 'barrack-like' dwellings diverted attention from the high standards which these early organizations set in terms of accommodation. Their dwellings were to be models in the true sense of that term, establishing the self-contained flat as the expectation for each family, and showing how proper standards of ventilation, water-supply and sewage-disposal could be achieved for low-wage earners. The standards of amenity were high for their day:

The earliest dwellings not only had sinks with constant water, inside water closets for each house, but dust shafts for the removal of rubbish and ashes as well. Some had gas-lighting, some had built-in ovens, ventilated meat safes, excellent cupboard space. They were not only more comfortable houses than working class people were used to, but a good deal better than most of the lower middle classes could find in big towns.[22]

Such standards inevitably raised the cost of dwellings, often beyond the reach of most working families, and in attempting to overcome the problem the Peabody Trust, from the 1870s onwards, concentrated on a policy of 'associated tenements' which provided sets of two or three rooms with shared lavatories and sculleries. However, if the basic concern remained to raise the standards of cleanliness of the working class, then this compromise had an obvious corollary: the rules and regula-tions controlling the tenants became stricter and more interventionist. Tenants were expected to be respectable, there were resident superintendents, buildings were locked at night, and private internal playground and drying areas were maintained. Such interference did not appeal to many working class families, who preferred the freedom of the slums; but, on the other hand, it provided a model of the way the respectable working class could benefit from housing reform.

These model dwellings were operated within the constraints of current social and economic beliefs. While concerned to improve the housing conditions of the urban poor, the companies and individuals providing these ventures sought a commercial return on their investments. As a result, building was not only basic, but the accom-modation allowed was restricted; the density of building on the ground and of people within the building was consequently high. The model schemes of the dwelling companies and housing societies provided healthy conditions, but did nothing to improve the urban environment. Tarn has argued that if the housing movement had flourished in a more aesthetically conscious age, such as the era of the early municipal garden suburban estates, then the effect might have been different.

However, in the 1860s and 1870s the limitations in concept and design, coupled with a wide spread of concern for the problem of overcrowding and the lack of planning, led housing reformers to seek a solution in a new form away from the town. It was increasingly recognized that if a housing programme for the working classes was to be successful it had to break away from the existing commercial and speculative arrangements and be ordered by more responsible architectural and sanitary controls.

It is necessary that in country districts near to our large towns, large numbers of small houses should be created for working people with a special arrangement made for their rapid conveyance to and from their place of labour. I am certain it would be attended with the most beneficial results for the health of our densely populated towns. It is no argument at all to say that working people employed in towns will not go to live in the suburbs. That is merely because they have not at present the accommodation to live there, nor the means of conveyance to and from their work at a low charge.[23]

The problem of transport, however, would not be such an important factor in the suburban expansion of provincial towns as it was in London. Thomas Beggs drew attention to this in 1866:

> The evils of overcrowding are most difficult in the Metropolis, and more difficult of treatment from the large areas covered by building of all kinds and the distance of the suburbs from any of the great centres. In Manchester, Birmingham and Leeds, notwithstanding the huge size of these towns, it is still practicable for the inhabitants to reach environs by an easy walk and if the dwellings be judiciously close to go home for the mid-day meal. There is still sufficient space around our large manufacturing towns to build cottages for the workmen without having recourse to large blocks of buildings such as have been erected in the Metropolis.[24]

The way was open in the provinces for the rapid development of working class housing according to the spatial demands of bye-laws and local building regulations. In London, the magnitude of the problem called for more far-reaching reform. It was this that attracted the attention of most housing reformers, and as a result the 1860s and 1870s saw the development of an ideal of suburban life for the working classes – of suburbs some distance from the centre of commercial activity and separated from existing development. In other towns, the nature of land use and its value meant that suburbs could simply serve to extend the existing built-up area, while in London the suburb had to be a separate entity.

At the 1866 meeting of the Social Science Association, H.W. Rumsey saw the answer to the problem of overcrowding in central housing districts in the reduction of densities on new housing-estates, which could only be achieved by means of escape to a suburban settlement on the penny train. At the same meeting, Thomas Worthington, the architect, urged the establishment of suburban villages wherever central sites were either too scarce or too costly. Like many, he drew attention to the activities of Titus Salt at Saltaire and the advantages of moving a whole community, works and residences together, away from the built-up area. In such schemes there was an element of control, which it was felt was necessary if the irresponsibility of the speculator was to be avoided. Likewise, James Hole indicated that, while the establishment of suburban communities was the desired aim, precautions must be taken to prevent the transfer of the urban slums to the outside. The new communities should be model villages laid out with due regard to health and comfort. Development could only be ensured by the co-operation of the railway companies to run cheap trains at suitable hours.

It was the inadequacy of transport facilities, however, which meant that, in the third quarter of the century, schemes for housing the working classes in the suburbs were not practical possibilities. But models were then formulated which matured late in the century, when the growing affluence and mobility of the artisans, combined with the increasing availability of transport made suburban living a viable alternative. The interest of the 1860s did, however, mean that several schemes for suburban estates were mooted which provided the precedents for the layout of organized estates of two-storey housing. The Metropolitan Association for Improving the Dwellings of the Industrious Classes experimented in South London with small estates of semi-detached cottages and gardens, and the Suburban Village and General Dwellings Company promoted model schemes of suburban dwellings with the following aims:

> . . . to provide, at the most rapid rate possible, healthy pleasant and comfortable abodes for the overcrowded population of the metropolis. The company will purchase estates in all the suburbs near to and having direct railway connection with London, and erect thereupon complete villages. The houses erected will contain from four to eight rooms with every domestic convenience, each house to have a piece of garden ground. Educational establishments, etc. will be provided and also a limited number of shops erected.[25]

Practical difficulties and financial considerations limited the implementation of this model. Nevertheless, such ideals took root in the housing reform movement of the time and influenced the whole development of housing and estate planning at the end of the nineteenth century. What was recognized was: 'The need to transplant the great masses of those living in the city to the immediate vicinity of the green fields.'[26]

This search for a rural environment was reflected in the attention now bestowed on the desirability of gardens and open spaces. These were seen, on the one hand, simply in terms of the benefits gained through a less crowded layout of housing; while on the other, they were envisaged as positive sources of physical and moral betterment. But in any case their provision was central to any scheme of suburban estate development. Sanitary and spatial considerations were here united. Describing his ideal city of health – Hygeia – Benjamin Richardson explained:

> Gutter children are an impossibility in a place where there are no gutters for their innocent delection. Instead of the gutter, the poorest child has the garden; for the foul sight and smell of unwholesome garbage, he has flowers and green sward.[27]

In practical terms, individual gardens were seen as antidotes to the evils of urban life and their cultivation a relief from the associated dangers. S. Broome reported to the Social Science Congress on the value of gardens to the poor:

> It is truly pleasing to see how much they seem to enjoy their bit of garden. They tell me it fills up all their leisure hours of a morning and evening; it keeps them from public houses in the evenings, and visitors coming to see the flowers find the house and children clean when they call. The next neighbours copy their example and so it passes from one to another. I already belong to twelve floral societies, numbering from 50 to 100 members each and not one shabby man amongst them. Very rarely do you find a man who is fond of flowers taken up for a misdemeanour of any kind.[28]

Thus housing reformers' attention was now directed towards the total environment. With increasing disillusionment in the construction of tenement blocks as the sole answer to the housing problem, greater stress was laid on the healthy as well as the aesthetically beneficial aspects of a natural environment. This was a cause which was furthered by and received most coherent justification from the work of George Cadbury and his achievements at Bournville.

From his knowledge of Birmingham, which extended throughout the Victorian period, and from his work with the Adult School Movement, Cadbury was convinced of 'the power of nature to touch the hearts of men', and of 'the purifying effects of cleansing contact . . . with the primal sanities of nature'.[29] With the establishment of Bournville, he was concerned not only to move his workforce out of the overcrowded and polluted atmosphere of the city, but also to provide the means and encouragement for them to benefit from the open space thus acquired. The trust deed for the village ensured that houses should not occupy more than one-quarter of their site, and that at least one-tenth of the land, in addition to roads and gardens, should be reserved for parks and recreation grounds. This pattern secured a pleasing aesthetic appearance for the front of the houses, along with privacy and economy at the rear.

Such environmental concerns in housing inevitably involved heavier expenditure on estate development. As such costs had to be met by the tenants, large numbers of working men were excluded from the benefits which Cadbury had anticipated. It was essential that certain economies in development and layout be incorporated before the visual models of Bournville and Port Sunlight could be transferred to the suburban estate, and that such concepts of planning be adopted in preference to customary speculative suburban growth. The catalyst that united the aesthetic and practical elements in a new approach to planning was Ebenezer Howard's *Garden Cities of Tomorrow*, first published in 1898. In that book Howard proposed the building in the heart of some agricultural district in England a town of 32,000 inhabitants where the most approved modern methods of engineering and sanitary science should be adopted, and the utmost attention devoted to securing healthy and beautiful houses and conditions of life and work for all classes of people. It was shown that there was a general consensus of opinion that the continued growth of large cities, combined with a decline in the population of the country districts, was an unhealthy development. The resulting problem, according to Howard, was how to create, in the midst of the fresh air of the country, opportunities for profitable investment and industry, and prospects of pleasant forms of social life more attractive than any to be found in the great towns and cities.

Apart from this approach, however, Howard's Garden City offered little that was novel either in design or thought. It reflected the pattern of utopian communities envisaged throughout the nineteenth century, and drew heavily on the ideas of earlier social reformers. It was probably this very eclecticism in Howard's thesis, however, that was its strength. Land nationalizers, co-operators, liberals, conservatives, fabians, socialists, anarchists and housing reformers were all attracted by some part of the theory. At the same time, the notion of the Garden City stimulated those men of business and government who were becoming increasingly disturbed by contemporary conditions of urban existence. The Physical Deterioration Committee reported in 1904 and, though the evidence and statistics did not establish that there was actual physical deterioration, they did nevertheless demonstrate the enormous proportion of 'unfits' in the population, and in particular made evident the havoc wrought by the modern city on the physical, mental and moral capacities of the people. It was also becoming evident that Britain's greatest rival in industry, Germany, was already making provision for the renewal of urban life by granting its municipalities powers to regulate the growth of the cities.

A stream of housing reformers visited Germany and brought back accounts of what was being done there. Motivated by Ebenezer Howard's book, the ever-increasing number of housing and town planning enthusiasts formed an association with the intention of developing a model town which, in surprisingly short time, was realized in the Garden City of Letchworth. However, few members of the Garden City Association looked for just one solution to the many social problems, and this resulted in a quiet watering-down of the thesis until it became synonymous in the public mind, and in the minds of many early planners, with the garden suburb.

Under the umbrella term of the Garden City Movement, however, reformers were united in supporting the improvement of existing towns on 'Garden City principles', and the planning of all land likely to be used for building. Whatever the differences of opinion about approach and emphasis, there was agreement on the benefits for housing of pre-planning. As Howard expressed it:

> The essential thing is that before a sod is cut or a brick laid, the area must in its broad outlines be properly planned with an eye to the convenience for the community as a whole, the preservation of natural beauties, the utmost degree of healthfulness and a proper regard to communication with the surrounding district.[30]

These new cencepts of planning and design were of particular importance in that they involved economies in construction and layout which made the model of housing estate development on Garden City lines a possible and realistic alternative to traditional speculative activity. Thus when housing and town planning was at last legislated for nationally in 1909, it was conceived of in terms of planned garden suburbs.

The new housing model of the twentieth century was not, therefore, a rejection of previous housing reform attitudes and endeavours in the nineteenth century, but rather an extension on those foundations which represented an assimilation of the experience of various practical achievements in housing reform over the previous sixty years.

Moreover, this was a model which, in the form of the suburban housing estate, incorporated a continuing Victorian ideal. It was a model that had filtered down from the aristocratic estate, through the extensive middle class villa estates, ultimately to the model working class suburban estate. This model had gained impetus, both locally and nationally, from the Victorians' reaction to urban living, and their increasing awareness of the virtues of fresh air and the need for open space. Its form was determined by a contemporaneous reaction to the housing conditions of the early nineteenth century, and more significantly by the reaction to the housing built under the first bye-laws with their concentration on sanitary reform.

The application of the suburban ideal to working class housing was made possible on the one hand by improvements in urban transportation and the slowly increasing affluence of the bulk of the working class, and on the other hand by the incorporation of new methods of estate layout and concepts of housing design. The latter were the culmination not of a process of national reform or legislation, nor indeed of any single strand of development; rather they owed their development and expression to the combination of a multitude of small and locally varying estate developments, and in particular to the combination of the concept of the industrial community with the planning, housing and financing exercises of the differing self-help bodies. This was the tradition on which the early planners of the Garden City Movement were able to draw; and it was the eclecticism of that movement in drawing so many disparate strands together that gave it its strength, and made the form of its development so attractive to a multitude of housing reformers, local authorities and, ultimately, national government.

It is also significant that the model that had gained common currency by the early twentieth century involved neither individual nor institutional patronage. It incorporated a model of a different kind: a model of finance as distinct from design. For the garden suburbs were largely the consequence of co-partnership activity, building on the tradition of Victorian self-help and encapsulating the experience of the building society movement, which saw itself as the vehicle for working people as a class solving their own housing problems. Such societies, particularly in the provinces, had during the nineteenth century been the means by which working class and middle class investors and mortgagees united for their mutual benefit. They enabled improvement through self-help in a way that Samuel Smiles had originally encouraged:

> The accumulation of property has the effect which it always has on thrifty men – it makes them steady, sober and diligent. It weans them from revolutionary notions and makes them conservative. When workmen by their own industry and frugality have secured their own independence, they will cease to regard the sight of others' well-being as a wrong inflicted on themselves; and it will no longer be possible to make political capital out of their imaginary woes.[31]

This model of thrift and security was the really practical housing model; it was the means of actually realizing improvement. The building societies did not involve themselves in the question of design or improvement of housing style. Indeed, there is no clear evidence that the standards applied by the building societies differed markedly from those adopted by ordinary builders. Their activities were concerned essentially with building investment, which by the time of the Royal Commission on Building Societies in the 1870s totalled over £32m. As a result the Commission recorded:

> They have promoted the investment in real or leasehold security, with very great safety on the whole, of several millions of money yearly; they have enormously encouraged the building of houses for the working and lower middle classes.[32]

This was a model which allowed those who, for financial reasons, could help themselves to do so and to overcome some of the problems which had beset the provision of working class housing in the nineteenth century. Through these means the better-off working man was able to aspire to middle class ethics and values. This was reflected not only in the pressure for house ownership, and status within the property-owning classes, but also in the desire to participate in the middle class exodus from town centres and to secure suburban respectability. The great contribution of the Garden City Movement was that, through the model of the garden suburb, it allowed the development of estates on which the upper working class and lower middle class were able to realize something of their arcadian dreams, and experience in modified form the lower density and informality of layout which had hitherto been the prerogative of their social superiors.

The garden suburb approach was reflected in the type of houses built, in the range of rentals, in the pattern of life on these estates, and primarily in their financial organization and promotion. The latter was commonly undertaken by means of tenant co-partnership which was the ultimate refinement of Victorian self-help in housing, for the co-partnership model combined corporate control with a personal interest in the profits arising from a right and economical use of property. Each tenant shareholder's share of the profits of the society was credited to him against the value of the house tenanted by him. By this means the tenant obtained the economic advantages arising from the ownership of his own house. At the same time, the society controlled the layout and design of the estate so as to secure pleasing architectural effects in the grouping and appearance of the houses, good quality building, and the limitation of the number of houses to the acre. Gardens and open spaces were a prevailing feature of these suburbs. Through this model it was possible to realize the hope of the promoters of the Garden City idea, that with the use of cheaper land, and with the introduction of less formal and thus less costly means of layout, it would be possible to build houses for working men that would not only be better designed, but would have a certain individuality and would 'look at least as well as middle-class houses'.

This housing pattern, like so many others of the nineteenth century, proved in practice more applicable to the needs of the better-off working-class and the lower middle-class. It was, however, this immediate practical appeal which ensured the ready acceptance of the Garden City idea, at least in its modified form as the garden suburb. The experimentation involved in this development at the beginning of the twentieth century led to the acceptance of new standards of layout and design in housing as being the proper standards for working-class housing after the First World War.

The problem with this dominant model, however, was that it did not provide a solution to the housing needs of the mass of the working class: those who were not able to distance themselves from their place of work, and those who could afford neither regular investment nor higher rents.

It was to overcome this problem that the Cheap Cottage Exhibition held at Letchworth in 1905 sought plans for houses that could be erected for less than £150 and so rent at well below 5s. per week exclusive of rates. This proved elusive, and the average 'rent' of houses on the co-partnership estates developed before the first world war ranged from 5s to 15s per week. This left the basic problem of improving the housing conditions of the poor unresolved.

By the early twentieth century no model had successfully tackled that dilemma. In the city centres the alternative improved model dwellings had significantly failed in this respect. At the end of the century an examination of the Peabody estates in London showed that the tenants were not the same class of people as those displaced by slum-clearance under the 1875 Cross Act. Without subsidy, the only possible means of overcoming this problem was, as Octavia Hill had long advocated, to lower the standard of accommodation. This the East End Dwellings Company, established in 1884, attempted to do. The main aim of the company was to provide for the poorest class of self-supporting labourers by accommodation of the very cheapest kind that would still return a fair rate of interest on capital.

Such rigid economy resulted in buildings of monumental grimness, which reinforced the poor's distaste for model dwellings. The necessity to provide water supplies and drains on a shared basis meant that the control over tenants' behaviour and habits was even more rigid than in the early blocks. The monotonous appearance of these dwellings was matched by the tight regulation of life within them. Despite these limitations, the East End Dwellings Company attempted to tackle the problem of housing the urban poor through slum clearance and re-building right up to the First World War. But by then it had departed from its original ideal and could only provide single-room tenements for the very poor if they were associated with more expensive accommodation and shops. What by then had become clear was the impossibility of providing dwellings for the very poor of a reasonable standard which were nevertheless economically realistic.

The necessities imposed by the limitations of economy and by the scale of demand combined with the developing architectural interest in simplicity and continuity in housing design and layout. Together they were reflected in the 'Memoranda' issued by the Local Government Board just before the First World War with regard to the provision and arrangement of houses for the working classes. This was the first time that central government had presented a model with positive advice concerning housing design and layout, as well as priorities in housing policy.

Hitherto, government had restricted itself to model bye-laws which were negative in terms of limiting certain types of development and laying down minimum standards. Now, in these Memoranda the Board summarized its views upon the more important principles applicable to the erection of separate houses or cottages and tenement dwellings in small houses. In the 1913 revision, it was laid down that, while it was desirable that simplicity of design and economy in construction should be aimed at, it would be well to bear in mind that houses erected by a local authority ought generally to be such as would be a model or standard for working men's houses erected by private persons. The standard of construction ought to be such that, with only a modest annual outlay for repairs, the houses would be capable of being maintained in a habitable condition for at least sixty years. The type of house regarded by the Board as most suitable was the self-contained house. Occasionally two-storey houses consisting of two self-contained dwellings might be required, but tenement-blocks were to be avoided. In general, the Board recommended a standard of ten houses to the acre as a basis for development, and suggested that, when the houses were to be built in rows, they should be set back from the street-line so as to allow for small gardens or forecourts between houses and the street. As a rule, it was considered that the number of houses in a continuous row should not exceed ten or twelve.

The Board admitted that the erection of detached or semi-detached cottages was somewhat more costly than the erection of cottages in blocks of four or more, but it conceded that, where the additional expenditure involved was justified, the arrangement might be of advantage. The Memoranda also suggested different layouts of streets and buildings which might reduce the expenditure on land and street-construction. These included the formation of groups of houses on backland, access to the houses being either from comparatively narrow streets, if the houses were set well back from the street line, or from streets of full width, of which portions might be turfed or planted with trees; the grouping of a number of houses round an open space, and the formation of a vehicular street at the back of the houses, leaving a stretch of garden-ground between the fronts of the houses and the footway.

These suggestions reflected the degree to which current concern with the overall concept of layout was reflected in official thinking, though it was still considered necessary to point out the dangers of building houses with unduly narrow frontages which meant that the required internal space had to be achieved by making the houses deep or with back projections. It was stressed, therefore, that in order to avoid interference with access of light and air to the rooms, the frontages should not be unduly restricted.

In conclusion, the Board intimated to local authorities that care should be taken to comply with the local bye-laws and statutory provisions in force in the district relating to streets, open spaces and new buildings. In a circular letter, however, the Board argued the importance of local authorities reviewing the requirements of their bye-laws so that, whilst prescribing reasonable provisions with a view to securing stability, protection from fire, and conditions essential to health, they should not be unduly restrictive in regard to the erection of small dwelling-houses.

The guidelines for the layout of working-class housing estates had been laid down and a code of practice established. By the First World War, local authorities had clearly assimilated the tenets of 'garden-city' or 'town-planning' design as then understood, and the earlier extravagances had begun to be tempered by awareness of the need for economy and simplicity. Official favour was bestowed on town planning of the kind advocated by Unwin. The visual norm of the suburban estate was now established as low-density housing with ample gardens and customarily tree-lined streets. There was also accepted the need for a greater variety of house types, rather than just the three-bedroomed model of earlier garden suburbs. The standards laid down by the Local Government Board were accepted and followed most closely in the recommendations of the Tudor Walters Committee, which advised on the construction and layout of working-class housing for post-war Britain.

By 1918, however, the problem was not so much one of style or character of layout for working-class housing estates, but rather how such were to be developed on the scale now required. During the course of the war the shortage of houses had risen steeply. The problem had been increasing since the Finance Act of 1910, but during the war the diversion of labour and materials from housing to war needs had worsened the situation. When the Tudor Walters Comittee reported, it estimated that at least 500,000 working-class houses were needed, in addition to which, in order to meet the requirements of the normal increase in population and to take the place of houses demolished, an annual supply of 100,000 new houses was needed. The Local Government Board had expressed its willingness to prepare schemes, subject to adequate state assistance, for about 258,000 houses.

It was held that a very large proportion of working-class houses must still depend on private enterprise of one kind or another, and, unless there was co-ordination of these various activities, little would be done in many districts, and rural housing was certain to be neglected because of the difficulty of creating sufficient local opinion to make the authorities act. It was clear that after the war private enterprise would be conducted under great difficulties because of high prices and the shortage both of labour and materials. The Committee was convinced that, unless there was some supreme guiding directive, an adequate housing programme was not likely to be carried out, but that rather the shortage of houses for some years after the war would increase rather than diminish. They consequently recommended the establishment of a strong housing department with two experienced and capable chief commissioners for England and Wales and for Scotland. It was further suggested that the country should be divided up into districts and local commissioners appointed who would work under central control yet have executive powers vested in them.

In the view of the Committee there was greater scope in housing for public-utility societies, which would be an important auxiliary to the work of the local authorities. The grouping of large employers in the industrial districts for the erection of villages planned on modern lines and developed on the outskirts of towns would be a great boon for the working classes, and would have the advantage of being carried out in the form of complete schemes. Public authorities as well as the tenants would be represented on the boards of management of such societies. The limitation of dividend upon the share capital, which was a condition of the formation of public-utility societies, prevented any exploitation of the tenants and rendered all surplus revenue, resulting from good management, available for promoting the amenities of the villages.

The Committee also considered that the whole question of land acquisition by public authorities for working-class dwellings, and the legislation under which it was then carried out, needed careful consideration and revision, both to achieve economy in price and to avoid unnecessary delays. It was further suggested that it would be worth considering whether local authorities might not supplement their own building operations by laying out suitable land, providing roads and sewers, and leasing it for private building schemes of an approved kind.

Though the Tudor Walters Committee considered the possibilities of housing developments by industrialists and public-utility societies – well tried supports of the Victorian housing-reform movement – its most important feature was the official weight given to the role of the public authority with regard to house-building and the recognition of the inevitability of subsidization. The demands of war had broken down resistance to the latter, while the enforced break in the housing cycle from 1914 to 1918 meant that the new scale of the problem called for a new response. Both local and professional opinion increasingly recognized the necessity of controlled municipal housing within the framework of a national policy. At a meeting of the Town Planning Institute in 1918, Percy Houfton, the architect of several model garden-village schemes, acknowledged this need:

> I think we shall have to rely more and more on municipal action. No-one, taking a dis-
> passionate view, can say that the speculative system has given anything but evil results,
> or that a drastic change is not urgently needed . . . there are difficulties to be overcome,
> but it is a question whether the competitive system has not over-reached itself, and
> whether the economies due to co-operation will now outweigh the economies which
> competition is supposed to secure.[33]

The fundamentals of the Victorian housing movement had been questioned, the pressures of war had enforced new responses. New methods of financing and control were to dominate housing development now. But its concept and style was still based on the environmental standards contained in the 1909 Town Planning Act, though the decade past had seen the maturing of new notions of planning and design. It was the combination of these two facets that the Tudor Walters Report enshrined and handed down. The war years had seen hesitant attempts to break out of the suburban trend, to rediscover the utopian community, or at least the original ideal of the Garden City. But in the end the garden suburb reigned supreme. By 1918 the housing debate had momentarily resolved itself and the way was set for the creation of 'one of the standard visual symbols of twentieth century Britain – the low-density council-housing estate'.[34]

This policy was put into practice through two Acts passed by the coalition government in 1919, which for the first time required local authorities to make plans for the provision of houses in their area. Through financial mechanisms the state took control of working-class housing, and introduced the control of council rents, with the result that these could now be established in relation to the ability of the tenant to pay rather than simply the cost of the property. The strict requirement of economic rents was abandoned. The result in terms of quantity was disappointing, and only 214,000 houses were planned under these provisions, compared with the estimated need of 500,000. The Addison Act did however establish the standards of space and facilities which had been brought forward in the Tudor Walters Report. A model was presented based on houses of the 'Garden-City' vernacular style, commonly grouped in blocks of four or six cottages and arranged informally around trees and greenery.

The policy underlying this model was changed in the Housing Acts of 1923 and 1924, with the tightening of financial controls and subsidies. But though the houses built under these Acts were less generously planned and equipped than the immediate post-war houses, nevertheless they maintained the model established. So for example, under the 1923 Chamberlain Act there was no major departure from the Tudor Walters layout and plans, though the average size of house was smaller. There was a preference for the non-parlour type house; cheaper drainage systems were used; the roof pitches were reduced, and economies were made in garden walls and fences. Under the Wheatley Act of 1924, which was operative until 1933, 508,000 houses were built, with subsidies, by nearly all the big local authorities. Such houses, however, constituted no more than a fifth of the total number of houses built in this period, when the main input came from speculative building. Their importance and significance lay in the fact that they served as exemplars of the general model established through the National Housing Manual.

Though economies in building were effected, it was seldom possible between the wars to erect houses to let at rents within the means of the lower-paid workers. In consequence the various Housing Acts included powers under which financial assistance, in the form of both state and rate aid, was made available to bridge the gap between interest returns and other charges and the rents which could be afforded.

These Acts also contained important provisions affecting the design of the working-man's home, such as limiting the density of development to eight houses to the acre in agricultural parishes and twelve per acre elsewhere, and regulating the floor area of rooms and the sizes of houses. In planning the site for houses, it was recognized that the roads should be governed by the contours of the land, natural features should be preserved and attention should be given to the aspect of the houses themselves. It was considered essential to provide a civic or social centre for the community, with a hall, library, churches, cinema and shops, as well as schools and recreation areas. Successful layout depended on the ease of access between houses and the social centres. At the same time, it was argued that the grouping of houses in blocks of six or eight would be more restful than the endless repetition of semi-detached dwellings. In building working-men's houses, the government advised that materials would receive heavy wear and tear, and therefore it would be false economy to use cheap materials. In designing the house, wastage of space should be avoided so that rooms of adequate size could be provided and the specified areas of the house would comply with the statutory requirements.

Under the 1923 Act the design model was a two-storey house with a minimum floor area of 620 and a maximum of 950 superficial square feet. By 1930 the specifications for individual rooms had been stabilized at 180 square feet for the living room and for the three bedrooms 150, 100 and 65 square feet, respectively. From 1923 onwards there was a statutory obligation to provide a fixed bath, which meant the installation of hot-and-cold-water circulating systems. It was also accepted that houses should be wired for electrical apparatus, as well as piped for gas, since it was cheaper to provide for both at the time of building rather than instal one after erection. Advice was given on the most satisfactory materials for external walling, for roofing and floors, on the respective advantages of sash and casement windows, and the character of doors and fittings. With this level of control, it was perhaps inevitable that some measure of standardization and similarity in planning should result, particularly in view of the tight financial restraints governing the erection of working-men's houses by local authorities under these Housing Acts. These houses tended to be either two-bedroomed or three-bedroomed non-parlour houses, or three-bedroomed parlour houses. Probably the most successful were those in which local traditions were followed and simplicity was the keynote of design.

The alternative model to this populist vernacular derived between the wars from both the European urban tradition and European artistic ideals. In England, with the ascendancy of the Garden City and the suburban housing model, the emphasis had been, in the early twentieth century and in the years after the First World War, on the family house placed within its garden setting. Housing within towns, and particularly in the form of multi-storey flats, had been condemned as being out of sympathy with the traditional expectations of the English working man. By the later 1920s, however, the flat movement was beginning to attract greater support from architects and designers who were influenced by the Modern Movement, and who had been excited by the workers' flats in Vienna and the possibilities they offered for imaginative construction and layout.

The Modern Movement's reaction against traditional styles was both stimulated and symbolized by Le Corbusier's *Vers une architecture* in 1923, which argued that the house should be designed functionally in response to the needs and requirements of the inhabitants. This philosophy was summarized by Ozenfant in *Foundations of Modern Art* (1928) when he wrote, 'The house, the box for living in, must before everything be serviceable: it is a machine that functions, a tool'.[35] Along with this went a freeing of architects and builders from traditional and structural constraints, with the development of revolutionary techniques in the use of steel frames and reinforced concrete.

Such ideas and innovations were changed into a realistic model after the national slum clearance campaign had been inaugurated by Greenwood's Housing Act of 1930. Prior to that, the majority of English cities did not use their powers of slum clearance, and in the 1920s confined their use of housing subsidies to suburban estates, without undertaking inner-city, multi-storey redevelopment. London and Liverpool continued the nineteenth-century tradition of tenement-building, and some other cities built a few blocks during the course of the 1920s; but these were not only very limited in number, but were also a continuation of the earlier concept of model dwellings. After 1930 the availability of subsidies for flat-building had the result that nearly all major cities built some flats before the outbreak of the Second World War, and in London flat-building exceeded cottage-building for the first time in 1931. In the course of this development, the style of flat-building changed from that of grim tenements, whose appearance was determined primarily by cheapness, to that of modernity with a properly-developed sense of concern for the standards of layout and design of fittings. Economic control, in the form of subsidies, combined with technical innovations, architectural ideals and social concern.

The result was the re-emergence of the old flat-versus-cottage controversy. Slum clearance encouraged a new idealism in the housing movement. Environmentalists supported it as a means of preserving the vanishing countryside, while social reformers and church leaders saw this as the best means of regeneration of slum-dwellers, without the necessary destruction of communities which the suburban alternative carried with it. About all this, there was, as Alison Ravetz has suggested, 'more than a touch of the millenarianism that inevitably accompanies reports of the newest architecture, while it is still clean, white and original'. It resulted, nevertheless, in the replacement of the simplified brick Georgian style deployed by many authorities by the architecture of the Modern Movement deriving from the experience of European cities.

The consequence was not just one of style, though that was evident in the use of curtain-walling and curved facades, of cantilevered balconies and eliptical arches, and flat roofs and flush windows; it was also one of internal planning and layout. This was the working out of the doctrine of functionalism and of the development of design from usage. To this end, Antony Bertram, one of the leading exponents of the idea of the house as a machine for living in, emphasized the importance of planning rooms in relation to one another and on the basis of requirement and demand. Rooms such as kitchens and dining-rooms were to be located for greatest practical convenience. Along with this concern for the needs of tenants went a heightened appreciation of the quality of living which, at blocks of flats such as Quarry Hill in Leeds, resulted in the installation of lifts and refuse-disposal systems, and the provision of shops, playgrounds, communal laundry and drying-rooms, crêche and community hall. Local authorities in the 1930s were attempting to change the image of flat-dwelling through the application of new standards of comfort, privacy and amenity.

The flat as a model, however, never really caught the public imagination, for the majority sought, and for the first time a great many were able to achieve, a suburban lifestyle which represented what Mumford has called 'the collective attempt to lead a private lifestyle'.[36] Speculative house-building did, perhaps, more than anything else to change the appearance of the country between the wars. It also extended the possibility of house-ownership, notably to white-collar workers but also to many higher-paid manual workers. Between 1919 and 1939, of the 3,998,000 new houses erected, 2,886,000 were privately built, such activity reaching a peak in the years 1935–39.

From a design point of view, these products of the building industry left much to be desired. Spreading out on available land at the edge of towns and cities, housing followed lines of communication in ribbon developments, and little attention was given to overall layout of estates, the provision of facilities, or the balance between town and country. Few of the houses were designed by architects, and they tended to be variations on a basic plan, which were enhanced and given a superficial individuality through the addition of various decorative features, such as imitation half-timbering, weather-boarding, tile-hanging, leaded lights and ornamental brick-work. In appearance and disposition, such speculative housing reflected a continuing romantic ideal, and through it a new first generation of house-owners achieved what J.M. Richards rightly saw as 'castles on the ground'.[37]

Though such developments flew in the face of both functionalist models and planning models, nevertheless they provided in their own way a model of individual interest and identity which continued the earlier nineteenth-century search for self-help and security. This was the model of house-ownership for a mass market. It was a model which, as in the nineteenth century, could not cater for the whole range of the working population, and certainly not for those in casual employment or facing the threat of unemployment. Speculative housing, acquired through mortgages, was aimed at those with a minimum regular salary of around £200 per year, and thus catered for skilled workers and lower-paid professionals who could meet outgoings of about £1 per week to secure a typical three-bedroomed semi-detached suburban house costing in the order of £650. Around this norm prices ranged from £250 to £1,250, and there was considerable variation in costs between different parts of the country. Through this activity, particularly in the 1930s, and with the arrangements between building societies and builders to make the process of house-acquisition both as simple and as painless as possible, the proportion of homes owner-occupied in England and Wales rose to 27 per cent by the time of the Second World War.

Along with the achievement of this financial opportunity, and closely related to the sense of independence which it engendered, went a new level of expectation with regard to the service and fittings demanded by the purchaser. Many of the features which had characterized the ideal homes of the post-First World War period, could now be incorporated in a practicable and realizable model for ordinary people:

> Prospective purchasers not only expected their houses to be brighter, cleaner, more comfortable and easily run than their parents' had been, but that amenity should go with appearance.[38]

Labour-saving had been part of the ideal home since the First World War, as instanced by the attention paid to that aspect of the housing question in the annual *Daily Mail* collections of ideal home plans. By the later 1930s such features had become an expected part of the speculative builders' model. This meant not only the inclusion of bathrooms with running hot-and-cold water, but also proper bathroom fittings; the provision of kitchens with sinks and draining-boards, cabinets and cupboards; the addition of gas-points and electric power-points in the main rooms; some system for heating water; the inclusion of a heated linen-cupboard and fitted cupboards; attention to the details of floor-surfaces, wall-decorations and window-fittings. The increased comfort and convenience which such features brought were becoming expected in the speculative model.

As a result, the suburban house, with its historical antecedents combined with its modern conveniences, became the aspiration and ambition of any who could afford to escape from the monotony of urban terraced housing. For such people, the individuality of their new homes and the lack of uniformity on the estates distinguished them socially and financially from contemporary municipal development. For many architects and planners, on the other hand, these very features were detrimental to the quality of such development, which seemed to be the very nega-tion of Howard's model of a garden city, and which reflected a lack of overall planning and authority.

It was in reaction to this situation that many designers and reformers in the 1930s renewed their attack on uncontrolled and undirected suburban expansion, and reformulated the model of mass housing within a concept of estate-development. This was argued for most cogently in the 1935 report of a Departmental Committee of the Ministry of Health on Garden Cities and Satellite Towns. This put forward the view that slum-clearance schemes were being undertaken with insufficient considera-tion of broad re-planning principles, and that suburban development was extended without the provision of adequate open spaces and playing-fields. Furthermore, while towns were expanding in an haphazard fashion, the patches of land between scattered suburban building were being filled in from time to time by fresh develop-ments which might have no relation to what had preceded them. This generally sporadic extension of building was not only costly as regards services, but also had the effect of destroying the amenities of the surrounding countryside. Such official dis-cussion took up the arguments of Trystan Edwards and Frederic Osborn and the movement gathering momentum for the building of new towns. Along with the broadening concept of town and country planning went a continuing concern for the layout of estates and the environs of the house. Such a model developed the notion of house-and-garden prevalent since the later nineteenth century and argued for a cohesive layout which conformed to some conscious design.

The effect in the 1930s was to apply what had become accepted practice in better-class estates to suburban developments of cheaper housing. Many controls, such as zoning and regulation of traffic, could be applied without adding to the cost of the houses. What was recognized was that a house could not be treated in isolation, but had to be conceived in terms of its neighbourhood development:

> . . . the chief emphasis must be placed on the desirability of . . . establishing houses with an agreeable environment within the means of the greatest number.[39]

Such a model depended, however, on external control. It follows a certain élitist notion that planning is done by experts, and is not undertaken either by or for the people most concerned. This view of the model house and improvement had generally prevailed throughout the preceding 100 years. The development of different approaches depended essentially upon realignment in social policy, for the traditional approach had under-rated the complexity of the interaction between social behaviour and the physical environment. Octavia Hill had begun to realize that com-plexity, and to emphasize the intangible relationship between what is designed and erected, and the use that is made of such structures. For the first time in the 1930s that variable was identified and investigated, and the basis established for the creation of a new form of model.

This was given substance shortly before and during the Second World War when Mass Observation undertook its extensive enquiry into people's homes. This survey was concerned not only to identify causes of complaint, but also to highlight those factors which were considered most important and desirable in the home for the future. The model that was clearly identified by popular demand was that of the small house in a garden with a considerable degree of privacy. The reaction against tenements and the need not only to share facilities in some cases, but even the enforced close contact with neighbours, was strongly felt. The concerns that pre-occupied earlier Victorian housing reformers were still prevalent.

It was not surprising, therefore, that the survey found most satisfaction amongst those who lived on the newer housing estates. This response was promoted not simply by the appeal of the surroundings of such houses and the desirability of a garden, but also out of preference for the facilities and conveniences which went with such houses. Most working-class families sought a three-bedroomed house, organized on two floors. Within that basic structure the survey identified the increasing desire to separate the sitting-room and the eating-room, to ensure that the bathroom was separate and on the upper floor, and to incorporate a properly fitted and well organized kitchen. As Burnett has concluded, 'Clearly the "fit" between people's preferences and what the better council-houses provided was a close one'.[40] The concerns of tenants and would-be tenants, were not so much to do with the overall organization or concept of the town and its environs, but much more to do with the practical reality of their 'ideal home' and its immediate surroundings. These were the continuing standards and aspirations of the lower-middle classes and skilled working classes.

These standards characterized much of the discussion and debate about housing policy and reconstruction during the Second World War, though that discussion and debate was conducted on a much broader basis than hitherto. By late 1941, a pre-occupation with the problems of social reform was apparent in all levels of society. Evacuation had made the upper and middle classes aware, often for the first time, of the continuing horror of slum-housing at the heart of large towns and cities. At the same time, destruction arising from enemy air-raids brought a new urgency to the unsatisfied housing requirements of London and other major cities. Houses required for people deprived of their homes through war amounted to more than one seventh of the pre-war total; these were added to the houses needed for people remaining in slums or living in overcrowded condition, for those not living in slums but in property which did not offer tolerable living conditions, and for young couples married during the war or shortly before who had never had a separate dwelling.

Contemporary accounts of these problems presented a situation which bore many of the hallmarks of the housing conditions of the previous century. The over-crowding survey of 1935–36 had shown that in England and Wales 3.8 per cent of the population were living in overcrowded conditions; in London this figure rose to 9.1 per cent and in parts of the East End to 24 per cent. These figures were, however, based on a very low definition of overcrowding as being a maximum of two persons per room in a dwelling. Many more millions of people were living in inadequate houses which, though not slums, did not offer satisfactory accommodation, and in which there were no bathrooms, sanitary arrangements were poor and many rooms were bug-ridden. Deprivation was still the lot of most working-class families.

These problems were followed through in various investigations during the course of the war and contributed to that gathering public sentiment which underlay the recommendations of the Beveridge Report in 1942. Of undoubted importance in that process was the increasing input from women. The war, though not changing fundamental social attitudes, did mean a new economic and individual freedom for women, and the experience of this could not be ignored. The participation of women and of other under-privileged classes in the community, along with the unparalleled destruction of the environment, gave rise to a firm determination to secure a better future than had been achieved after the First World War. This was evident in many aspects of social reform, but nowhere more clearly than in housing which, conceived as part of the overall concept of the welfare state, was to be planned both in the interests of individual welfare and with a view to the improvement and ultimate transformation of society.

In these circumstances, it was both timely and necessary that the model for post-war housing should be examined. The government contemplated a housing programme of between three and four million to be built in the ten to twelve years following the war. This entailed doubling the rate of building during the inter-war period, when four million houses were built in twenty years, with approximately three million being provided by private enterprise and one million by local authorities. From the outset, it was envisaged that in the post-Second World War housing programme the proportion of houses built by local authorities would be larger, and that indeed authorities might be required to provide up to two million houses during the first decade.

Contemplating the scale of development necessary, the government and the Housing Advisory Committee recognized that since the First World War local authorities had had to build five times the number of houses contemplated by the Tudor Walters Committee, with the result that frequently the development of municipal housing estates had become distorted by the growth of vast one-class residential districts.

The reaction to this was an emerging concept of planning which involved the creation of independent or semi-independent mixed social communities provided with all the industrial, social and other activities and amenities on which community life depended. At the same time, there had been changes of outlook and habit affecting the design and equipment of houses themselves. The previous quarter of a century had seen a steady rise in the general standard of living and a growing desire for, and appreciation of, good housing and, in particular, of convenient demestic arrangements and labour saving fittings. This tendency was bound to continue after the war, as housing was expected to keep abreast of the extension of education and serve as a further means of social security. Moreover, it was recognized that the experience gained by the vast number of women in industry and in the services had influenced their attitude to housing; for war-time factories and hostels often provided higher standards of services and equipment which made women intolerant of inferior conditions in their own homes.

In the same way, both men and women had become conscious during the war of the practicalities of modern scientific developments and expected to enjoy the benefits of these discoveries at home. The broad extension of public services between the wars, in terms of piped water, electricity and gas, had brought changes in domestic habits, particularly with regard to appliances for cooking and the consequent nature and design of the room in which cooking was undertaken. These developments reinforced the view that the most important question in designing and equipping dwellings was that of how a house was run and the use made of the various rooms.

As a result, pre-eminent attention was given in the post-war housing model to the consolidation of 'good design'. This implied good layout, good internal arrangements, good equipment and good appearance. It was considered to be lack of design that had hitherto provided so much dreary and monotonous development throughout the country. At the same time the evidence of various enquiries and investigations showed a widespread, if not always clearly articulated, dissatisfaction with this state of affairs and an innate desire for well-ordered and pleasant surroundings.

Design was recognized as a function of the architect, and in the past too little use had been made of trained architects in the planning and design of housing estates, despite the growing attention given to the subject in both architectural writing and training. It was realized as a requirement that all authorities should employ trained architects in connection with their housing schemes, and that central government through the Ministry of Health should prepare manuals of illustrated plans for the assistance of local authorities and their architects. This would be essential if new housing was to be undertaken with the intention of adding positively to the beauties of the town and countryside.

The notion of model housing was thus firmly placed in the orbit of central government in the post-war period. Government, at the same time, had come to recognize the significant future role of town and country planning, and the need to perceive housing within a broader social and economic context. Many serious mistakes were recognised in the planning and layout of housing during the inter-war period. In particular, problems had arisen from the over-rigid separation of private and public housing; insufficient attention had been given to the provision of churches, schools, club buildings, shops, open spaces and other amenities; the location of residential estates too far from places of employment had occasioned long and expensive journeys to work; too strict an interpretation of density zoning had resulted in insufficient variety of types of dwellings; a failure to appreciate the value to a neighbourhood of good design had affected not only the houses themselves but also their setting.

With the recognition of these problems and under the stimulus of war, especially through the shattering of cities by bombing, town and country planning came to concern itself with fundamental problems of social and economic life. Housing was now examined against the major needs of whole communities and in relation to the daily lives of the total population. Different areas and different functions of the city were studied in relation to the whole. Such concerns were articulated in the 1941 National Planning Basis, subsequently incorporated in the Town and Country

Planning Act of 1947, and reflected in the work of the New Towns Committee. Housing policy and practice was finally and firmly linked with government responsibility for the location of new industry and the decentralization of population.

Such considerations confirmed the role of the model as a source not only of information but also of instruction, of both ideas and of direction. Through the work of the New Towns Committee, and central guidance on the layout, administration and appearance of new estates, government influenced the context in which housing was conceived and subtly controlled the expectations of society. There was as yet no Ministry of Housing, but there had developed through the Ministry of Health an authority with the powers which enabled it to take a full view of the problem and to plan the necessary work.

In the aftermath of the Second World War, housing and the housing problem would no longer be treated in isolation from town planning, transport, public services, education, social amenities, the location of industry and the re-organisation of the building industry. The policy of first the coalition government and then, more particularly, the post-war Labour government, led to the definition of the social principles and standards on which housing was to be based in the future. This involved a change from any sense of operating on different, and thereby lower, standards for the working classes, and from the notion that authority was simply seeking to ameliorate the situation; it was replaced by an outright acceptance of the priority that future housing must be raised to the standard of the highest modern levels of building and equipment, and must be related to an overall policy of land use and control. In practice, this meant a concern for environment and community:

> Caught up in the spirit of socialist euphoria, many architects and planners saw themselves as social engineers whose principal, and complementary, tasks were to create community and beauty, to reunite the social classes which the nineteenth century had divided, by restoring the town as a natural and desirable organ of civilised life.[41]

After the Second World War, the model for housing development was backed by determination to build more houses and better houses than had resulted in the years after the First World War. Yet despite the high hopes that there was opening a new chapter in the history of housing standards, the situation was essentially a continuation of early expectations. The foundations remained the legacy of the nineteenth century. The previous decades of development of low-density housing had established the need for both state subsidization and the involvement of local government in the building process. What had come to fruition in post-war Britain was a well nurtured sense of responsibility with regard to working-class housing, and a sense of responsibility for a healthy populace which was directly linked to a prevailing concept of beauty as being fundamental to good housing. Though the reality of the suburban experience was being questioned in the light of new architectural thinking and social responsibility, the ideal that derived from nineteenth-century housing reform remained inviolate, and for the general public the potency of that model remained implicit in the residential desirability of low density development.

NOTES

1. Price, U. (1798) *Essay on the Picturesque*, **11**, p. 405.

2. Loudon, J.C. (1840) *The Cottagers' Manual of Husbandry, Architecture, Domestic Economy and Gardening*, p 3.

3. Marshall, J.D. (1968) Colonisation as a factor in the planning of towns in north-west England, in Dyos, H.J. (ed.) *The Study of Urban History*, p. 220.

4. Gaskell, P. (1836) *Artisans and Machinery*, London: J.W. Parker, p. 303.

5. McDouall, P.M. (1842) *An Exposure of the Tricks of Thomas Ashton Esq, passim*.

6. Akroyd, E. (1862) *On Improved Dwellings for the Working Classes*. London, p. 6.

7. Dodd, W. (1842) *The Factory System Illustrated*. London: Cass Reprint, 1968, p. 89.

8. Faucher, M.L. (1844) *Manchester in 1844*, p. 112.

9. Rollinson, S. (1873/4) *Transactions of the Chesterfield and Derbyshire Institute of Engineers*, **VI**, p. 142.

10. Hole, J. (1866) *The Homes of the Working Classes with Suggestions for their Improvement*. London, p. 80.

11. Akroyd, *op. cit.*, p. 4.

12. *Transactions of the National Association for the Promotion of Social Science*, 1857, p. 440.

13. *Ibid.*, 1864, p. 514.

14. *Ibid.*, 1873, p. 455.

15. Mile End Old Town Medical Officer of Health, *Annual Report*, quoted in Jephson, H., (1907) *The Sanitary Evolution of London*, p. 227.

16. *The Times*, 29 April 1862.

17. *Transactions of the National Association for the Promotion of Social Science*, 1874, p. 597.

18. *The Times*, 29 April 1862.

19. *The Architect*, **XIV**, 1875, p. 342.

20. Tarn, J.N. (1971) *Working-Class Housing in Nineteenth-Century Britain*. London: Lund Humphries, p. 21.

21. Tarn, J.N., (1968/69) The Peabody Donation Fund. *Architectural Association Quarterly*, Winter, p. 32.

22. Gauldie, E., (1979) *Cruel Habitations*. London: Allen & Unwin, p. 221.

23. *Transactions of the National Association for the Promotion of Social Science*, 1864, p. 585.

24. *Ibid.*, 1866, p. 620.

25. *The Builder*, **XXV**, 1867, p. 231.

26. *Ibid*, **XXVI**, 22 Aug 1868 supplement, p. xi.

27. *Transactions of the National Association for the Promotion of Social Science*, 1875, p. 107.

28. *Ibid.*, 1858, p. 641.

29. Gardiner, A.G. (1923) *Life of George Cadbury*. p. 12.

30. Quoted in MacFadyen, D. (1933) *Sir Ebenezer Howard and the Town Planning Movement*. Manchester: Manchester University Press, p. 129.

31. Quoted in Price, S.J. (1958) *Building Societies: Their Origin and History*. London: Franey, pp. 139–140.

32. *Royal Commission on Building Societies, Second Report*, 1873, para. 54.

33. *The Architect and Contract Reporter, c.* 1918, p. 290.

34. Ashworth, W. (1959) *Genesis of Modern British Town Planning*, London: Routledge & Kegan Paul, p. 196.

35. Ozenfant, A. (1931) *Foundations of Modern Art* (English edition). p. 137.

36. Mumford, L. (1961) *The City in History*. London: Secker & Warburg, p. 486.

37. Richards, J.M. (1946) *The Castles on the Ground: The Anatomy of Suburbia*. London: Architectural Press.

38. Burnett, J. (1978) *A Social History of Housing 1815–1970*. Newton Abbot: David & Charles, p. 225.

39. Adams, T. (1934) *The Design of Residential Areas*. Cambridge, Mass.: Harvard University Press, p. 18.

40. Burnett, *op. cit.*, p. 232.

41. *Ibid.*, pp. 279–80.

Bibliography

A. OFFICIAL PUBLICATIONS

UK government. (Note BPP = British Parliamentary Papers. The roman numerals after the letters BPP and the date of the session refer to the number of the volume in the series as bound for the House of Commons.)

Report of the Select Committee on the Health of Towns, BPP, 1840, **XI**.

Poor Law Commissioners, *Report on an Inquiry into the Sanitary Condition of the Labouring Population of Great Britain*, 1842.

First Report of the Royal Commission on the State of Large Towns and Populous Districts, BPP, 1844, **XVII**.

Second Report of ibid., BPP, 1845, **XVIII**.

First Report of the Royal Sanitary Commission, BPP, 1868–9, **XXXII**.

Second Report of ibid., BPP, 1871, **XXXV**, and 1874, **XXXI**.

Interim Report of the Select Commission on Artizans' and Labourers' Dwellings Improvement, BPP, 1881, **VII**.

Final Report of ibid., BPP, 1882, **VII**.

Report of the Royal Commission on the Housing of the Working Classes, BPP, 1884–5, **XXX** and **XXXI**.

Report of the Joint Select Commission of the House of Lords and House of Commons on Housing of the Working Classes, BPP, 1902, **V**.

Report of the Inter-Departmental Committee on Physical Deterioration, BPP, 1904, **XXXII**.

Local Government Board, *Statistical Memoranda and Charts Relating to Public Health and Social Conditions*, BPP, 1909, **CIII**.

Local Government Board, *Report on back-to-back houses by Dr L W Darra Muir*, BPP, 1910, **XXXVIII**.

Local Government Board, *Report of the Committee on Building Construction in connection with the Provision of Dwellings for the Working Classes in England and Wales, and Scotland*, BPP, 1918, **VII**.

Local Government Board, *Manual on the Preparation of State-aided Housing Schemes*, 1919.

Ministry of Health, *Interim Report of the Committee to Consider and Advise on the Principles to be Followed in Dealing with Unhealthy Areas*, 1920.

Ministry of Health, *Report of the Departmental Committee on Housing*, BPP, 1932–3, **XIII**.

Ministry of Health, *Housing Manual on the Design Construction and Repair of Dwellings*, 1927.

Ministry of Health, *Report of the Departmental Committee on Housing*, BPP, 1932–3, **XIII**.

Ministry of Health, *Housing Act 1930 Re-Housing Operations: Typical Plans of Tenements and Other Dwellings*, 1933.

Ministry of Health, *Report of Departmental Committee on Housing*, 1933.

National Housing Committee, *National Housing Policy*, 1934.

Ministry of Health, *Report of the Departmental Committee on Garden Cities and Satellite Towns*, 1935.

Ministry of Health, *Interim Report of Departmental Committee on the Construction of Flats for the Working Classes*, 1935.

Ministry of Health, *Memorandum on Housing (Financial Provisions) Act*, 1938.

Ministry of Health, House Management and Housing Associations Sub-Committee of the Central Housing Advisory Committee, *The Management of Municipal Housing Estates*, 1938.

Report of the Royal Commission on the Distribution of the Industrial Population, BPP, 1939–40, **IV**.

Ministry of Works, *Housing Equipment*, 1944.

Ministry of Health, *Housing Manual*, 1944.

Ministry of Health, Design of Dwellings Sub-Committee of the Central Housing Advisory Committee, *Design of Dwellings*, 1944.

Ministry of Town and Country Planning. *Interim, Second Interim and Final Reports of the New Towns Committee*, BPP, 1945–6, **XIV**.

Central Housing Advisory Committee, *The Appearance of Housing Estates*, 1948.

Ministry of Housing and Local Government, *The Design of Residential Areas*, 1953.

Ministry of Housing and Local Government, *Design in Town and Village*, 1953.

B. PERIODICALS

The Architect
Architects' Journal
Architectural Review
The Builder
Building News
The Co-operator
Country Life
The Garden City
Journal of the Town Planning Institute
Quarterly Review
RIBA Journal
Town and Country Planning
Town Planning Review
Transactions of the National Association for the Promotion of Social Science

C. ARTICLES IN PERIODICALS

Bracebridge, T.H. (1857) On building cottages. *Transactions of the National Association for the Promotion of Social Science*.

Cameron, C.H. (1881) Results of the Town Labourers Dwellings Acts. *Transactions of the National Association for the Promotion of Social Science*.

Chamberlain, J. (1883) Housing of the poor. *Pall Mall Gazette*.

Chamberlain, J. (1883) Labourers and artizans' dwellings. *Fortnightly Review*, new series.

Chancellor, F. (1876) Improved dwellings for the working classes. *The Builder*, **XXXIV**.

Checkland, O. & S. (1975) Housing policy: the formative years. *Town Planning Review*, **XLVI**.

Cooper, N. (1967) The myth of cottage life. *Country Life*.

Cooper, N. (1967) The design of estate cottages. *Country Life*.

Costelloe, B.F.C. (1898/99) The housing problem. *Transactions of the Manchester Statistical Society*.

Daunton, M.J. (1980) Miners' houses: South Wales and the Great Northern Coalfield 1880–1914. *International Review of Social History*, **XXV**.

Dent, J.D. (1871) The condition of the British agricultural labourer. *Journal of the Royal Agricultural Society of England*.

Foyle, A.M. (1953) Henry Roberts, 1802–1876, a pioneer of housing for the labouring classes. *The Builder*, **CLXXXIV**.

Gatcliff, C. (1875) Improved dwellings and their beneficial effects. *Journal of the Statistical Society*, **XXXVIII**.

Hill, O. (1861) Cottage property in London. *Fortnightly Review*, no. XXXVI.

Hill, O. (1866) An account of a few houses let to the London poor. *Transactions of the National Association for the Promotion of Social Science*.

Hill, O. (1883) Common sense and the dwellings of the poor, improvements now practicable. *Nineteenth Century*, **XIV**.

Hill, O. (1884) Colour, space and music. *Nineteenth Century*, **XV**.

Honeyman, J. *et al.* (1900) Working-class dwellings. *Journal of the R.I.B.A.*, 3rd series, **VII**.

Jones, W. (1873) On the best plan of construction and arrangement of an agricultural labourer's cottage. *Transactions of the National Association for the Promotion of Social Science*.

Mann, P.H. (1952) Octavia Hill: an appraisal. *Town Planning Review*, **XXIII**.

Marshall, A. (1884) The housing of the London poor. Ways and means. *Contemporary Review*, **XLV**.

Papworth, J.W. (1857) On houses as they were, as they are, and as they ought to be. *Journal of the Society of Arts*, **V**.

Parker, B. (1928) Economy in estate development. *Journal of the Town Planning Institute*, **XIV**.

Peppler, S. (1981) Ossulston Street: early LCC experiments in high-rise housing 1925–9. *London Journal*, **VII**.

Pevsner, N. (1943) Model houses for the labouring classes. *Architectural Review*, **XCIII**.

Pevsner, N. (1959) LCC housing and picturesque tradition. *Architectural Review*, **CXXVI**.

Pollard, S. (1964) The factory village in the Industrial Revolution. *English Historical Review*, **LXXIX**.

Reynolds, J. (1948) The model village of Port Sunlight. *Architect's Journal*.

Richards, J.M. (1936) Sir Titus Salt. *Architectural Review*, **LXXX**.

Robinson, G.T. (1871/22) On town dwellings for the working classes. *Transactions of the Manchester Statistical Society*.

Marquis of Salisbury (1883) Labourers' and artizans' dwellings. *National Review*.

Torrens, W.M. (1879) What is to be done with the slums? *Macmillan's Magazine*.

Tarn, J.N. (1969) Housing in Liverpool and Glasgow: the growth of civic responsibility. *Town Planning Review*, **XXXIX**.

Tarn, J.N. (1965) The model village at Bromborough Pool. *Town Planning Review*, **XXXV**.

Tarn, J.N. (1968) Some pioneer suburban housing estates. *Architectural Review*.

Tarn, J.N. (1968/69) The Peabody Donation Fund. *Architectural Association Quarterly*, Winter.

Vivian, J. (1912) Garden cities, housing and town planning. *Quarterly Review*, **CCXVI**.

D. BOOKS AND PAMPHLETS

Abercrombie, L.P. (1939) *The Book of the Modern House*. London: Hodder & Stoughton.

Adams, M.B. (1912) *Modern Cottage Architecture*, 2nd ed. London: Batsford.

Adams, T. (1932) *Recent Advances in Town Planning*. London: G. & A. Churchill.

Adams, T. (1934) *The Design of Residential Areas*. Cambridge, Mass.: Harvard University Press.

Adshead, S.D. (1923) *Town Planning and Town Development*. London: Methuen.

Akroyd, E. (1862) *On Improved Dwellings for the Working Classes*. London.

Aldridge, H.R. (1915) *The Case for Town Planning. A Practical Manual*. London: National Housing and Town Planning Council.

Aldridge, H.R. (1923) *The National Housing Manual*. London: National Housing and Town Planning Council.

Aldridge, H.R. (1925) *The Extent and Character of the National Housing Needs*. Manchester: Cooperative Union.

Allen, G. (1919) *The Cheap Cottage and Small House*. London.

Anthony, H. (1945) *Houses: Permanence and Prefabrication*. London: Pleiades Books.

Armytage, W.H.G. (1961) *Heavens Below*. London: Routledge & Kegan Paul.

Artizans & General Properties Company Ltd (1967) *Artizans Centenary, 1867–1967*. London.

Ashworth, W. (1954) *The Genesis of Modern British Town Planning*. London: Routledge & Kegan Paul.

'B., B.' (1910) *Co-Partnership in Housing*. London.

Balgarnie, R. (1877) *Sir Titus Salt. Baronet. His Life and His Lessons*. London: Hodder & Stoughton.

Barley, M.W. (1961) *The English Farmhouse and Cottage*. London: Routledge & Kegan Paul.

Barnes, H. (1923) *Housing: the Facts and the Future*. London: Ernest Benn.

Barnes, H. (1934) *The Slum: Its Story and Solution*. London: King.

Barnett, H. (1928) *The Story of the Growth of Hampstead Garden Suburb, 1907–1928*. London.

Bateman, R.A. (1925) *How to Own and Equip a House*. London: R.A Bateman Ltd.

Bauer, C. (1935) *Modern Housing*. London: Allen & Unwin.

Bauer, C. (1952) *Social Questions in Housing and Town Planning*. London: University of London Press.

Bell, C. & R. (1972) *City Fathers, The Early History of Town Planning in Britain*. Harmondsworth: Penguin.

Benevolo, L. (trans. Landry, J.) (1967) *The Origins of Modern Town Planning*. London: Routledge & Kegan Paul.

Bertram, C.A.G. (1935) *The House, A Machine for Living In: A Summary of the Art and Science of Homemaking Considered Functionally*. London: Black.

Bournville Village Trust (1941) *When We Build Again*. London: Allen & Unwin.

Bournville Village Trust (1949) *Landscape and Housing Development*. London: Batsford.

Bournville Village Trust (1956) *1900–1955*. Bournville: Bournville Village Trust.

Bouverie, M.F.P. (1944) *Daily Mail Book of Post War Homes*. London: Associated Newspapers.

Bowkett, T.E. (1843) *Freehold Property for Mechanics*. London: Cleave.

Bowley, M. (1945) *Housing and the State, 1919–1944*. London: Allen & Unwin.

Bowmaker, E. (1895) *The Housing of the Working Classes*. London: Methuen.

Boyson, R. (1970) *The Ashworth Cotton Enterprise*. Oxford: Clarendon Press.

Briggs, M.S. (1937) *How to Plan Your House*. London: English Universities Press.

Briggs, M.S. (1944) *Building Today*. London: Oxford University Press.

British Broadcasting Corporation (1945) *Homes for All*. Worcester: Littlebury and Co.

Brooks, S.H. (1839) *Designs for Cottage and Villa Architecture*. London: Thomas Kelly.

Buckingham, J.S. (1849) *National Evils and Practical Remedies*. London: Peter Jackson.

Burnett, J. (1978) *A Social History of Housing 1815–1970*. Newton Abbot: David and Charles.

Cadbury, G. (1915) *Town Planning with special reference to the Birmingham Schemes*. London: Longman.

Cadbury Brothers Ltd (1922) *Bournville Housing*. Bournville.

Caird, J. (1851) *English Agriculture in 1850–1851*. London: Longman.

Casson, H.M. (1946) *Homes by the Million*. Harmondsworth: Penguin.

Chambers, G.F. (1881) *The Law Relating to Public Health*, 8th ed. London: Stevens.

Chapman, S.D. (ed.) (1971) *The History of Working Class Housing*. Newton Abbot: David & Charles.

Clarke, J.J. (1920) *The Housing Problem: Its History, Growth, Legislation and Procedure*. London: Pitman.

Cleary, E.J. (1965) *The Building Society Movement*. London: Elek.

Collier, F. (1965) *The Family Economy of the Working Classes in the Cotton Industry, 1784–1833*. Manchester: Manchester University Press.

Creese, J.L. (1966) *The Search for Environment*. New Haven: Yale University Press.

Cullingworth, J.B. (1963) *Housing and Local Government in England and Wales*. London: Allen & Unwin.

Culpin, E.G. (1914) *The Garden City Movement Up-to-Date*. London: Garden Cities and Town Planning Association.

Curl, J.S. (1983) *The Life and Works of Henry Roberts*. Chichester: Phillimore.

Daily Herald (1946) *Daily Herald Modern Homes Exhibition Catalogue*. London.

Daily Mail (1919) *Ideal Workers' Homes*. London.

Daily Mail (1920) *Daily Mail Ideal Labour-saving Home*. London.

Daily Mail (1922) *The Daily Mail Bungalow Book*. London.

Daily Mail (1927) *Daily Mail Ideal Houses Book*. London.

Daily Mail (1946) *Daily Mail Ideal Home Book*. London.

Daily Mail (1923, further eds. 1937, 1939, 1950) *Daily Mail Ideal Home Exhibition Catalogue*. London.

Daily Mirror (1913) *The Perfect Home and How to Furnish It*. London.

Denby, E. (1938) *Europe Re-housed*. London: Allen & Unwin.

Dewsnup, E.R. (1907) *The Housing Problem in England: its Statistics, Legislation and Policy*. Manchester: Manchester University Press.

Dodd, W. (1842) *The Factory System Illustrated*. London. (Cass Reprint, 1968).

Donnison, D. (1960) *Housing Policy since the War*. Welwyn: Codicote Press.

Dyos, H.J. (1966) *Victorian Suburb*. Leicester: Leicester University Press.

Dyos, H.J. (ed.) (1968) *The Study of Urban History*. London: Arnold.

Dyos, H.J. & Wolff, M. (1973) *The Victorian City: Images and Realities*. London: Routledge & Kegan Paul.

Edwards, A.E. (1981) *The Design of Suburbia*. London: Pembridge.

Elsas, M.J. (1942) *Housing Before the War and After*. London: King & Staples.

Engels, F. (1969) *The Condition of the Working Classes in England*. London: Panther.

Fabian Society (1900) *The House Famine and How to Relieve It*. London.

Festival of Britain (1951) *Guide to the Exhibition of Architecture, Town Planning and Building Research*. London: HMSO.

Fletcher, B.F. (1871) *Model Houses for the Industrial Classes*. London: Longman.

Fussell, G.E. (1949) *The English Rural Labourer: his home, furniture, clothing and food from Tudor to Victorian times*. London: Batchworth Press.

Gaskell, P. (1836) *Artisans and Machinery*. London: J.W. Parker.

Gaskell, S.M. (1983) *Building Control: National Legislation and the Introduction of Local Bye-Laws in Victorian England*. London: Bedford Square Press.

Gatcliff, C. (1854) *Practical Suggestions on Improved Dwellings for the Industrious Classes*. London.

Gatcliff, C. (1875) *On Improved Dwellings and their Beneficial Effect on Health and Morals, and Suggestions for their Extension*. London.

Gauldie, E. (1974) *Cruel Habitations: A History of Working-Class Housing, 1780–1918*. London: Allen & Unwin.

Geddes, P. (1915) *Cities in Evolution*. London: Williams & Norgate.

George, W.L. (1909) *Labour and Housing at Port Sunlight*. London: Alston Rivers.

Giedion, S. (1948) *Mechanization Takes Command. A Contribution to Anonymous History*. New York: Oxford University Press.

Gloag, J. (1970) *Mr. Loudon's England*. London: Oriel.

Godwin, G. (1859) *Town Swamps and Social Bridges*. London (Reprinted 1972: Leicester University Press.)

Godwin, G. (1864) *Another Blow for Life*. London.

Greater London Council (1978) *Home Sweet Home: Housing designed by the London County Council and Greater London Council Architects, 1888–1975*. London.

Hampstead Garden Suburb Trust (1937) *The Hampstead Garden Suburb: Its Achievements and Significance*. Hampstead.

Hampstead Tenants Limited (1907) *Cottages with Gardens for Londoners*. London.

Harris, G.M. (1905) *The Garden City Movement*. Hitchin: Town and Country Planning Association.

Harvey, W.A. (1906) *The Model Village and Its Cottages: Bournville*. London: Batsford.

Havinden, M.A. (1966) *Estate Villages*. London: Lund Humphries.

Higgs, M. (1902) *Glimpses into the Abyss*. London: King.

Hill, O. (1883) *Homes of the London Poor*. London: Macmillan.

Hill, W.T. (1956) *Octavia Hill*. London: Hutchinson.

Hole, J. (1866) *The Homes of the Working Classes, with suggestions for their Improvement*. London.

Holroyd, A. (1871) *Saltaire, and its Founder, Sir Titus Salt, Bart. 2nd ed.* Saltaire.

Horsfall, T.C. (1904) *The Improvement of the Dwellings and Surroundings of the People: The Example of Germany*. Manchester: Citizens' Association for the Improvement of the Dwellings of the People.

Horsfall, T.C. (1908) *The Relation of Town Planning to National Life*. Wolverhampton.

Hosking, W.H. (1848) *A Guide to the Proper Regulation of Buildings in Towns, as a means of Promoting and Securing the Health, Comfort and Safety of the Inhabitants*. London.

Howard, E. (ed. Osborn, F.J.) (1946) *Garden Cities of Tomorrow*. London: Faber.

Howkins, F. (1926) *An Introduction to the Development of Private Building Estates and Town Planning*. London: Estates Gazette.

Hughes, V.M. (1959) *History of the Growth and Location of the Corporation's Housing Schemes*. Sheffield.

Jephson, H. (1907) *The Sanitary Evolution of London*. London: Fisher Unwin.

Jevons, R. and Madge, J. (1946) *Housing Estates*. Bristol: University of Bristol.

Kay, J.P. (1832) *The Moral and Physical Condition of the Working Classes Employed in the Cotton Manufacture in Manchester*. Manchester: James Ridgeway.

Labour Publications Department (1934) *Up with the Houses! Down with the Slums!* London.

Lever, W.H. (1902) *The Buildings Erected at Port Sunlight and Thornton Hough*. London.

Local Government Act Office (1858) *Forms of Bye-Laws under the Local Government Act for the Guidance of Local Boards in the preparation of Bye-Laws*. London.

Local Government Board (1883) *Knight's Annotated Bye-Laws*. London.

London County Council (1901) *The Housing Question in London*. London: London County Council.

Loudon, J.C. (1836) (new ed. 1842) *An Encyclopaedia of Cottage, Farm & Villa Architecture and Furniture*. London: Longman.

Loudon, J.C. (1838) *The Suburban Garden and Villa Companion*. London: Longman.

Lumley, W.G., & E. (1876) *The Public Health Act, 1875*. London: Shaw.

McDouall, P.M. (1842) *An Exposure of the Tricks of Thomas Ashton Esq. A New Whig Magistrate and an Old Cotton Lord. Or the truth about the Delicacies and Luxuries of the Paradise at Hyde*. Manchester.

MacFadyen, D. (1933) *Sir Ebenezer Howard and the Town Planning Movement*. Manchester: Manchester University Press.

Madge, J. (1945) *The Rehousing of Britain*. London: Pilot Press.

Madge, J. (ed.) (1946) *Tomorrow's Houses: New Building Methods, Structures and Materials*. London: Pilot Press.

Madge, J. (1948) *Human Factors in Housing*. London: Bureau of Current Affairs.

Manchester Diocesan Conference (1902) *Report of the Committee appointed to consider the Question of the Housing of the Poor*. Manchester.

Manchester Sanitary Committee (1904) *Housing of the Working Classes: History of the Schemes and Description of the Corporation's Dwellings*. Manchester.

Marcroft, W. (1884) *A Co-operative Village: How to Conduct it and Where to Form It*. Manchester: Central Co-operative Board.

Martin, A. (1906) (new ed. 1909) *The Small House*. London: Alston Rivers.

Maslen, T.J. (1843) *Suggestions for the Improvement of Our Towns and Houses*. London.

Mass Observation Survey (1943) *Enquiry into People's Homes*. London.

Masterman, C.F.G. (1909) *The Condition of England*. London: Methuen.

Meakin, B. (1905) *Model Factories and Villages: Ideal Conditions of Labour and Housing*. London: T. Fisher Unwin.

The Ministry of Health (1939) *About Housing*. London.

The Ministry of Works (1944) *Housing Equipment*. London.

Morgan, J.M. (1850) *The Christian Commonwealth*. London: Phoenix.

Mumford, L. (1961) *The City in History*. London: Secker & Warburg.

National Dwellings Society (1887) *Homes of the London Working Classes: Philanthropy and five per cent.* London.

National House-Builders' Registration Council (1938) (Further eds. 1939, 1946, 1949) *Model Specification approved by the National House-Builders' Registration Council.* London.

National Housing and Town Planning Council (1910) *1900–1910: A Record of Ten Years Work for Housing and Town Planning Reform.* Leicester.

National Housing and Town Planning Council (1929) *A Policy for the Slums.* London.

Nettlefold, J.S. (1908) *Practical Housing.* Letchworth: Garden City Press.

Nettlefold, J.S. (1914) *Practical Town Planning.* London: St Catherine Press.

Osborn, F.J. (1942) *New Towns After the War*, 2nd ed. London: Dent.

Osborn, F.J. & Whittick, A. (1963 new eds. 1969, 1977) *The New Towns.* London: Leonard Hill.

Parker, B. & Unwin, R. (1901) *The Art of Building a Home.* London: Longman.

Parker, F. (1955) *George Peabody, 1795–1809. Founder of Modern Philanthropy.* Nashville: George Peabody College for Teachers.

Parker, V. (1970) *The English House in the Nineteenth Century.* London: Historical Association.

Pearson, J.H. (1905) *Suburban Houses.* London: Spon.

Perry, C.A. (1939) *Housing for the Machine Age.* New York: Russell Sage.

Pevsner, N. (1960) *Pioneers of Modern Design*, rev. ed. Harmondsworth: Penguin.

Phillips, R.R. (1923) *The House You Want.* London: Country Life.

Phillips, R.R. (1936, new ed. 1939) *Houses for Moderate Means.* London: Country Life.

Phillips, R.R. (1937) *The Modern House and its Equipment.* London: Chadwick Trust.

Pollard, S. (1968) *The Genesis of Modern Management.* Harmondsworth: Penguin.

Price, S.J. (1958) *Building Societies: their Origin and History.* London: Franey.

Purdom, C.B. (ed.) (1921) *Town Theory and Practice.* London: Benn.

Purdom, C.B. (1925) *The Building of Satellite Towns.* London: Dent.

Reid, H.G. (1895) *Housing the People; an Example of Co-operation.* Paisley: Gardner.

Reiss, R.L. (1919) *The Home I Want.* London: Hodder & Stoughton.

Reiss, R.L. (1924) *The New Housing Handbook.* London: King.

Reiss, R.L. (1937) *British and American Housing.* New York.

Reiss, R.L. (1945) *Municipal and Private Enterprise Housing.* London: Dent.

Richards, J.M. (1946) *Castles on the Ground: the Anatomy of Suburbia.* London: Architectural Press.

Richardson, B.W. (1876) *Hygeia, a City of Health.* London.

Ritchie, J.E. (1853) *Freehold Land Societies.* London.

Roberts, H. (1850) *The Improvement of the Dwellings of the Labouring Classes.* London.

Roberts, H. (1851) *The Model Houses for Families.* London.

Roberts, H. (1859) *Improvement of the Dwellings of the Labouring Classes.* London.

Roberts, H. (1862) *Essentials of a Healthy Dwelling*. London.

Rowntree, B.S. & Pigou, A.C. (1914) *Lectures on Housing*. Manchester: Victoria University.

Rubinstein, D. (1974) *Victorian Homes*. Newton Abbot: David and Charles.

Savage, W.G. (1915) *Rural Housing*. London: T. Fisher Unwin.

Sayle, A. (1924) *The Houses of the Workers*. London: T. Fisher Unwin.

Scott, G.G. (1857) *Remarks on Vernacular Architecture, Present and Future*. London: Murray.

Scott, G.G. (1879) *Personal and Professional Recollections*. London: Sampson Low.

Scott, M.H. Baillie (ed.) (1910) *Garden Suburbs. Town Planning and Modern Architecture*. 2nd ed. London: Fisher Unwin.

Scottish Housing Advisory Committee (1948) *Planning Our New Homes*. Edinburgh.

Sennet, A.R. (1905) *Garden Cities in Theory and Practice*, 2 vols. London: Benrose.

Sharp, T. (1932) *Town and Countryside: Some Aspects of Urban and Rural Development*. Oxford: Oxford University Press.

Sheffield Corporation (1905) *Handbook of Workmen's Dwellings*. Sheffield.

Simon, E.D. (1923) *Houses for All*. London: New Way Series.

Simon, E.D. (1945) *Rebuilding Britain – A Twenty Year Plan*. London: Gollancz.

Simon, E.D. & Inman, J. (1935) *The Rebuilding of Manchester*. London: Longman.

Smalley, G. (1909) *The Life and Times of Sir Sidney Waterlow*. London: Edward Arnold.

Smith, E. (1875) *The Peasant's Home, 1760–1865*. London.

Smith, E.J. (1918) *Housing: The Present Opportunity*. London: King.

Smith, T. (ed.) (1951) *Daily Mail Ideal Home Exhibition House Plans*. London: Daily Mail.

Society for Improving the Condition of the Labouring Classes (1851) *Plans and Suggestions for Dwellings*. London.

Society for Improving the Condition of the Labouring Classes (1851) *Plans and Descriptions of Model Dwellings*. London.

Solly, H. (1884) *Home Colonisation: Rehousing of the Industrial Classes: or Village Communities v. Town Rookeries*. London: Sonnenschein.

Solly, H. (1884) *Industrial Villages: a Remedy for Crowded Towns and Deserted Fields*. London.

Sparrow, W. Shaw (ed.) (1904) *The British Home of Today*. London: Art and Life Library.

Stewart, C. (1952) *A Prospect of Cities*. London: Longman.

Stewart, C.J. (1900) *The Housing Question in London, 1855–1900*. London: London County Council.

Strickland, C.W. (1864) *On Cottage Construction and Design*. Cambridge.

Sutcliffe, A. (ed.) (1974) *Multi-Storey Living: The British Working Class Experience*. London: Croom Helm.

Swenarton, M. (1981) *Homes Fit for Heroes: The Politics and Architecture of Early State Housing in Britain*. London: Heinemann.

Tarn, J.N. (1971) *Working Class Housing in Nineteenth Century Britain*. London: Lund Humphries.

Tarn, J.N. (1973) *Five Per Cent Philanthropy: An account of housing in urban areas between 1840 and 1914*. London: Cambridge University Press.

Thompson, F.L. (1923) *Site Planning in Practice*. London: Oxford Technical Publications.

Thompson, W. (1903) *The Housing Handbook*. London: National Housing Reform Council.

Thompson, W. (1907) *The Housing Handbook Up-to-Date*. London: National Housing Reform Council.

Tilley, M.F. (1947) *Housing the Country Worker*. London: Faber.

Townroe, B.S. (1924) *A Handbook of Housing*. London: Methuen.

Unwin, R. (1902) *Cottage Plans and Common Sense*. London: Fabian Tract.

Unwin, R. (1912) *Nothing Gained by Overcrowding! How the Garden City Type of Development may Benefit both Owner and Occupier*. London: King.

Vivian, H. (1908) *Co-Partnership in Housing in its Health Relationship*. London: Co-Partnership Tenants.

Walters, J. Tudor (1927) *The Building of Twelve Thousand Houses*. London: Ernest Benn.

Waterhouse, P. & Unwin, R. (1912) *Old Towns and New Needs: also The Town Extension Plan: being the Warburton Lectures for 1912*. Manchester: Manchester University Lectures.

Watson, A. (1966) *Price's Village*. Bromborough Pool: Price's (Bromborough) Ltd.

Weaver, L. (1919) *The Country Life Book of Cottages*, 2nd ed. London: Country Life.

Welwyn Association (1929) *Welwyn Garden City: Its Meaning and Methods*. Welwyn.

Whitten, R.H. & Adams, T. (1931) *Neighbourhoods of Small Homes*. Cambridge, Mass.: Harvard City Planning Studies.

Whittick, A. (1943) *Civic Design and the Home*. London: Faber.

Whittick, A. (1947) *The Small House: Today and Tomorrow*. London: Crosby Lockwood.

Williams, R. (1893) *London Rookeries and Colliers' Slums*. London: W. Reeves.

Worthington, T.L. (1893) *The Dwellings of the Poor and Weekly Wage Earners in and around Towns*. London: Swan Sonnenschein.

Yerbury, J.E. (1913) *A Short History of the Pioneer Society in Co-operative Housing*. London.

Yorke, F.R.S. (1934, later eds. 1943, 1944, 1948) *The Modern House*. London: Architectural Press.

Yorke, F.R.S. & Gibberd, F. (1937, later eds. 1948, 1950) *The Modern Flat*. London: Architectural Press.

Yorkshire Agricultural Society (1862) *Cottage and Farm Architecture*. York.

Young, T. (1934) *Becontree and Dagenham*. London.

Index